DELICIOUS!

C O L L E C T I O N

Simple Recipes
For Healthy Living

Recipes compiled and edited by
Sue Frederick, Editor
Laurel Kallenbach, Managing Editor
Gloria Bucco, Associate Editor
Kathryn Arnold and Carol O'Sullivan, Assistant Editors
Delicious! Magazine

◆

NEW HOPE COMMUNICATIONS INC.
BOULDER, COLORADO

New Hope Communications Inc.
1301 Spruce Street
Boulder, Colorado 80302

Library of Congress Cataloging-in-Publication Data
The Delicious! collection : simple recipes for healthy living /
  recipes compiled and edited by Sue Frederick.
     p. cm.
  Includes index.
  1. Low-fat diet. I. Frederick, Sue.
  RM237.7.D45 1992
  641.5'63—dc20   92-7881
                                                       CIP

ISBN 0-9632623-0-0

Designed by Maryl Swick
Cover photo by Russell McDougal

Printed in the United States of America

10 9 8 7 6 5 4 3 2 1

This book is dedicated to
our loyal Delicious! Magazine readers.

Table Of Contents

A Delicious! Gift To You

Dear Readers,

We offer this cookbook as a gift of love to our loyal *Delicious! Magazine* readers and newfound friends. Since its inception in 1985, *Delicious! Magazine* has published more than 500 recipes using wholesome natural foods. Here, we've selected the most tempting, healthy, quick dishes from our recipe files — as well as classics we often receive reprint requests for.

And of course, this book is for anyone who may not have seen *Delicious! Magazine.* We're convinced that when you skim through our collection and try these tasty, wholesome recipes, you'll become a *Delicious!* fan.

What is *Delicious! Magazine*? Put simply — we care about your good health. Our magazine is full of information to help you design a wholesome diet and live a healthy life. We feature articles from scientists such as nutritional biochemist Jeffrey Bland, Ph.D., on the link between diet and childhood I.Q., diet and women's hormones and other current research findings. Our wholesome recipes reflect this cutting-edge nutrition research as well as the latest culinary techniques for reducing dietary fat, cholesterol and sodium.

We believe that by eating the foods we've included, you may be able to prevent disease and stay healthy. That's our philosophy — live well and practice prevention. Here's to your long, healthy life!

Sue Frederick

Sue Frederick, Editor, *Delicious! Magazine*

Introduction

Natural food or "health food" has changed over the years. No longer are lentils and brown rice the only choices for healthy eating (thank goodness)! Our recipes are good for you, yet they taste and look terrific, too. Plus, most can be whipped up in 30 minutes or less. So if you're trying to change to a healthier diet, let our recipes be your gentle guides. Without sacrificing taste, you'll soon be eating more of what's good for you and less of what you want to avoid.

Why Low Fat?

The American Heart Association suggests a diet that contains 30 percent fat calories or less. Many studies, including the China Health Project, the largest epidemiological study ever done, are proving that a very low-fat, plant-based diet may help prevent cancer, osteoporosis and heart disease. Although most Chinese get just 7 to 10 percent of their dietary protein from animal products (the rest comes from vegetables, grains and beans), those who consume more animal protein have higher rates of heart disease and cancer, according to study results. In contrast, Americans typically get up to 70 percent of their protein from animal products and have much higher rates of heart disease than their Eastern neighbors.

Two of the most important factors contributing to heart disease are cholesterol and fat. Cholesterol is a waxy substance that occurs naturally in our bodies. Humans manufacture cholesterol in their livers for use as building blocks for sex hormones, cell membranes and digestive secretions. The body makes plenty of cholesterol for all its needs, but when we eat animal products, all of which contain cholesterol, an excess results. This excess accumulates as "plaque" along artery walls, eventually constricting blood flow and increasing the risk of heart attack.

The average American has a blood cholesterol level of 211 mg. % (211 milligrams of cholesterol in 10 milliliters of blood). The level recommended by the National Heart, Lung and Blood Institute (NHLBI) is 200 mg. % or less. However, in populations that have little coronary disease, the average level is 150 mg. %, which leads many physicians and other medical professionals to advocate even lower levels than those suggested by the federal government.

Not only does eating animal products increase cholesterol in our bodies, it adds saturated fats, which stimulate the liver to manufacture more cholesterol. Beef, chicken and other animal fats are largely saturated and should be eaten in moderation.

Vegetable oils are different, however. They are high in polyunsaturated and monounsaturated fats and are generally believed to decrease cholesterol levels. Currently, most Americans consume twice as much saturated fat as poly- and monounsaturated fats. The American Heart Association recommends that we include equal amounts of saturated, polyunsaturated and monounsaturated fats in our diets. To help you incorporate these diet guidelines, we've designed a "*Delicious!* Do's And Don'ts" chart (page 11) and a "Clarifying Natural Oils" chart (page 12).

Low-Fat & Loving It!

We're convinced that most Americans will be changing their diets in the next few years. We'd like to help make the change as tasty and enjoyable as possible. We've marked our heart healthy, low-fat recipes with a ♥ to draw your attention to dishes that fit into this healthier way of eating. Be sure to check our index for these low-fat, heart-healthy recipes when you're planning meals. We've also analyzed the fat content of each recipe to help you keep track of how much fat you're consuming.

Healthy cooking need not be bland. Indeed, a variety of delicious herbs and natural flavorings along with ingredients naturally low in saturated fats, sugars and salt can be found at your natural foods store. These will inspire you to create fabulously rich and tasty meals. For ideas to get you started, check our "Creative Flavor Boosters" (page 13).

We've included recipes containing chicken or fish in moderate portions, while others use soy-based protein products such as tempeh and tofu, which are cholesterol-free and low in saturated fat. If you've never cooked with soyfoods, consult our "Soy! Oh Soy!" chart (page 123) for tips on preparing and using a variety of soy products.

In addition, you'll find some *Delicious!* classics such as our Yin-Yang Tofu Cheesecake (page 205). Even though this recipe can't be considered low-fat, we know that everyone splurges occasionally. Just try to keep your overall daily intake of fat calories down to 30 percent of the day's total even when you enjoy a scrumptious creamy dessert. To keep tabs on how much of your caloric intake derives from fat, use the formula explained in "Go Figure" (page 11).

We wish you good health and happy eating!

Figuring Fat From Labels

When reading a food label, use these guidelines to quickly assess fat content of a single serving:

FOR ENTREES	FAT CONTENT
0-9 grams of fat	low
10-15 grams of fat	medium
> 15 grams of fat	high

Because desserts have a higher percentage of fat calories than other foods, evaluate them by these standards:

FOR DESSERTS	FAT CONTENT
0-4 grams of fat	low
5-6 grams of fat	medium
> 6 grams of fat	high

Delicious! Do's & Don'ts

So what should you eat? Follow these simple guidelines for improving your diet.

DO	DON'T
Eat less fat. Read food labels and avoid foods with more than a few grams of fat per serving — the fewer the better.	Forget to limit your intake of fat to less than 30% of your total daily calories.
Eat less meat and dairy products and eat more fruits, vegetables, grains and beans.	Eat more than 300 mg. of cholesterol daily.
Use natural vegetable oils, which are poly- and monounsaturated.	Use animal-based oils such as butter and lard, which are high in saturated fats and cholesterol.
Eat bread, pasta and baked goods made with high-fiber whole grains.	Eat products made with refined flours or processed grains, such as white bread.
Eat foods made with natural sweeteners like honey, molasses, granulated cane juice and rice syrup.	Eat foods made with refined sugar.
Eat more organic foods.	Eat foods grown with chemical fertilizers and pesticides.
Substitute salt-free herb seasonings, nutritional yeast, gomasio (ground sesame seeds) and powdered kelp (sea vegetable) for table salt.	Eat processed foods that are loaded with sodium or table salt, which is almost pure sodium chloride.

Go Figure!

We encourage you to read product labels when you shop for ingredients. The easiest way to assess the fat content is to determine fat percentage for each serving. The formula works like this:

Multiply the number of grams of fat by 9 (the number of calories in a gram of fat), then divide the result by the total number of calories.

For example, if an 8-ounce serving of soy milk has 127 calories and 5 grams of fat, it contains 35 percent of its calories from fat. (5 grams of fat X 9 = 45; 45 divided by 127 calories = .35 or 35 percent fat calories.)

Clarifying Natural Oils – A User's Guide

The American Heart Association recommends that we include equal amounts of saturated, polyunsaturated and monounsaturated fats in our diets. Animal fats are highly saturated whereas vegetable oils are low in saturated fats. Here we compare the fatty acid composition of natural vegetable oils.

OIL	TASTE & PROPERTIES	CULINARY USES	FATTY ACID COMPOSITION
ALMOND	Strong, toasted nut; low smoke point; not suitable for deep frying	Excellent in salad dressing, chicken salad or drizzled over fish; nut-flavored baked goods	Monounsaturated 64% Polyunsaturated 29% Saturated 7%
CANOLA	Light, clear, bland; high smoke point; all-purpose	Blends well for mayonnaise and dressings; especially good for baking	Monounsaturated 62% Polyunsaturated 32% Saturated 6%
CORN	Pleasant, "corny" flavor; general use	Good for baking — especially pie crusts — cooking and making popcorn	Monounsaturated 25% Polyunsaturated 62% Saturated 13%
OLIVE	Distinctive, fruity; not suitable for deep frying; all-purpose	Good for frying, sautéing, salad dressings, pasta sauces, some baking	Monounsaturated 77% Polyunsaturated 9% Saturated 14%
PEANUT	Slightly heavy, nutty; may "flash" at high temperatures	Excellent in Oriental stir-fries, Thai and Indonesian dishes; also good for salads	Monounsaturated 48% Polyunsaturated 34% Saturated 18%
SAFFLOWER	Fairly bland; good for frying since it does not foam; general use	Frying, sautéing, salad dressing, baking; use to dilute stronger oils; mayonnaise	Monounsaturated 13% Polyunsaturated 78% Saturated 9%
SESAME	Toasted sesame has a rich, strong flavor, and untoasted is lighter, more bland	Use toasted in salad dressings, Oriental dishes; untoasted for stir-fries	Monounsaturated 42% Polyunsaturated 44% Saturated 14%
SUNFLOWER	Nearly tasteless and odorless; all-purpose	Good in salads, stir-fries; use for frying, sautéing; mayonnaise; use to dilute stronger oils	Monounsaturated 21% Polyunsaturated 68% Saturated 11%

Note: The fatty acid composition of oils varies from source to source. Most of the fatty acid information in this chart is from the *Harvard Medical School Health Letter*, November 1987, and the *UC Berkeley Wellness Letter*, March 1987.

Creative Flavor-Boosters

*Cooking with a low-fat consciousness means adding flavor in creative ways.
We've found the following natural pantry staples indispensable
for stirring pleasure into simple meals and snacks.*

- Natural bottled **salsa** is virtually fat-free and low in salt. Besides enhancing Mexican dishes, salsa spices up scrambled tofu, dips (made with tofu and nonfat yogurt), beans, steamed vegetables and sandwiches.

- **Grainy mustard** flavored with herbs, wine, wasabi or miso is another wise choice. Whisk it with lemon juice to make an appealing sauce for fish or grains or with plain nonfat yogurt to top asparagus or broccoli. Try it instead of mayonnaise on whole wheat pita club sandwiches.

- **Salt-free seasoning blends** come in a variety of flavors such as French, Italian, Indian curry and Mexican. Give a generous shake to casseroles, plain rice or other grains, salads and vegetables.

- **Natural fruit juice** is another flavor enhancer. Use it for baking, basting, poaching and marinating. A citrus juice marinade will produce a juicy, moist chicken breast, while apple juice can be substituted for milk in baked goods. (Just use ¾ cup juice instead of 1 cup milk.)

- **Natural soup/sauce mixes** made with nonfat dry milk add a rich flavor to many dishes. Whisk a packet with nonfat yogurt for a flavorful dip or stir into brown rice for a unique pilaf. Mixed with low-fat milk or water, they are transformed into a sauce for plain chicken or fish. Look for them in a wide assortment of flavors from black bean to creole.

- Flavorful **vinegars** such as balsamic, raspberry, umeboshi plum and herb or pepper laced vinegars make delicious fat-free dressings for green, grain or pasta salads. You'll never miss the oil that's in bottled dressings.

- **Oriental sauces** such as tamari, shoyu, Szechwan, sukiyaki and teriyaki add a kick to lots of dishes. Shake a dash into stir-fries, dips, marinades and soup bases.

- **Other natural flavor boosters:** Miso, sea vegetables, pickled ginger, sun-dried tomatoes, lemon and orange peel, garlic, alcohol-free beer or wine, sauerkraut and pickle juice.

Where's The Fat?

Living a low-fat life-style means gaining an awareness of fat and cholesterol in the foods you eat. So how do foods stack up when it comes to fat? This chart gives a clear picture of the fat and cholesterol contents of common foods.

SERVING OF FOOD	CALORIES	GRAMS OF FAT	% OF CALORIES FROM FAT	MG. OF CHOLESTEROL
4 ounces of:				
Lean beef tenderloin	252	12.7	45	95
Boneless, skinless chicken breast	196	5.0	23	96
Fish (sole or flounder)	104	1.4	12	54
Tofu, firm	164	10.0	55	0
Tempeh	224	8.8	35	0
Whole egg (2 large eggs)	188	13.0	63	426
Egg whites (of 3 large eggs)	57	0	0	0
1 ounce of:				
Cheddar cheese	110	9.0	74	30
Soy cheddar	70	5.0	64	0
Feta cheese	75	6.5	59	25
Part skim mozzarella	80	5.0	56	15
½ cup of:				
Cottage cheese, 4% fat	120	5.0	38	17
Cottage cheese, 1% fat	90	1.0	10	5
Low-fat ricotta cheese	143	7.0	44	35
Cream cheese	434	44.0	91	125
Sour cream	208	20.0	87	40
Kefir cheese	264	24.0	82	0
Nonfat yogurt	60	0	0	0
1 teaspoon of:				
Butter	34	3.8	100	10
Margarine	34	3.8	100	0
Vegetable oil	40	4.5	100	0

SERVING OF FOOD	CALORIES	GRAMS OF FAT	% OF CALORIES FROM FAT	MG. OF CHOLESTEROL
1 tablespoon of:				
Peanut butter	100	8.0	72	0
Tahini	85	8.0	84	0
Miso	36	1.0	28	0
Tamari	11	0	0	0
Vinaigrette dressing	83	9.0	98	0
Catsup	16	0	0	0
Mustard	14	1.0	64	0
Mayonnaise	110	12.0	98	5
Tofu mayonnaise	40	4.0	90	0
1 cup of cooked:				
Whole-grain pasta	174	.6	3	0
Black beans	226	1.0	4	0
Brown rice	218	1.6	7	0
Whole wheat couscous	192	2.0	9	0
Quinoa	436	7.8	16	0
½ cup of:				
Dairy ice cream, vanilla	150	8.0	48	30
Soy frozen dessert	120	7.0	52	0
All-fruit sorbet	80	0	0	0
1 ounce of:				
Semi-sweet chocolate chips	150	8.0	48	0
Carob chips, unsweetened	140	7.0	45	0
Almonds	167	14.8	80	0
Potato chips	150	10.0	60	0
Pretzels	110	2.0	16	0
Popcorn, air popped	90	1.0	10	0
Raisins	82	.1	1	0
Apple slices	16	.2	11	0
Carrot sticks	12	.1	8	0

Sources: *Handbook of the Nutritional Value of Foods in Common Units*, prepared for the United States Department of Agriculture by Catherine Adams, Dover Publications, Inc., New York and *The Complete Book of Food Counts* by Corinne Netzer, Dell Publishing, New York.

The Delicious! Menu Planner
A WEEK OF WHOLESOME, LOW-FAT & SIMPLE MEALS

MONDAY

Breakfast	*Lunch*	*Dinner*
Granola Baked Pears With Fruit Glaze (p. 22)	Bombay Tomato Bisque (p. 117)	Tangy Tandoori Bake (p. 135) or
Sprinter's Ginseng Smoothie (p. 218)	Smoky Lentil Pâté (p. 52)	Protein-Packed Indian Pancakes (p. 153)
	Rice Cakes And Crudités	Hurry-Curry Vegetables (p. 154)

TUESDAY

Heavenly Quinoa Hash (p. 30)	Mushroom-Parsley Pita Sandwich (p. 168)	Chickpea Pasta Platter With Rosemary (p. 132)

WEDNESDAY

Blue Horizon Fruit Cakes (p. 29)	Nori Roll-Ups (p. 151)	Neapolitan Polenta Pie (p. 160)
Blueberry Preserves	Celestial Miso Soup (p. 115)	Dairy-Free Caesar Salad (p. 71)

THURSDAY

Bagel & Smoked Salmon With Pimiento Deli Spread (p. 32)	Hot Tabouli To Go! (p. 163)	Tempeh Tahiti With Brown Rice (p. 149)
		Snowy Lemon Mousse (p. 199)

FRIDAY

Apple Carrot Gems (p. 39)	Oat Bran Tuna Salad (p. 98)	Oriental Bean Cakes (p. 152)
Protein Punch Shake (p. 217)	Fresh Fruit	Stir-Fried Vegetables

SATURDAY

Banana Raisin Oat Bran Waffles (p. 25)	One Terrific Tofu Burger (p. 166)	Tic-Tac-Tortilla Stacks (p. 156)
	Peppy Potato Salad (p. 83)	Rice Latino (p. 86)

SUNDAY

Eggless Country Scramble (p. 21)	Fragrant Fish Fillets In Foil (p. 139)	Summer Squash Soup With Curry (p. 116)
Herbed Biscuit Twists (p. 47)	Tomato-Couscous Ring (p. 162)	Gingered Carrot Salad
Tomato Marimba (p. 228)	Yin-Yang Cheesecake (p. 205)	With Rice Cakes (p. 79)

Healthy Habits

While you may be cooking healthier meals at home, it's still tempting to grab a fast-food hamburger for lunch or a bag of chips and a soda for an afternoon snack. Instead, try these nutritious alternatives to popular high-fat, sugar-filled foods.

INSTEAD OF:	TRY:	INSTEAD OF:	TRY:
ALL-BEEF HOT DOG	Tofu hot dog	DAIRY ICE CREAM	Low-fat, nondairy soy frozen dessert; frozen yogurt, all-fruit sorbet
GROUND BEEF HAMBURGER	Burgers made with natural grains, vegetables, tofu and tempeh	POPSICLES	Popsicles made with unsweetened fruit juice, frozen bananas
ITALIAN SAUSAGE PIZZA	Whole-grain crust pizza topped with soy mozzarella and turkey sausage	MILKSHAKES	Fruit flavored kefir, amazake, yogurt smoothie
POTATO CHIPS	Flavored rice cakes (barbecue, teriyaki, cinnamon apple), popcorn seasoned with nutritional yeast, toasted tortilla or pita bread chips	PUDDING	Nonfat yogurt, amazake
		CHOCOLATE & CHOCOLATE SYRUP	Carob powder, date-sweetened carob chips, carob syrup
COLAS AND COMMERCIAL SODAS	Natural sodas, fruit juice spritzers	CANDY	Fresh or dried fruit, trail mix, fruit leather, honey sesame crunch bars, low-fat granola bars
SUGAR-COATED CEREALS	Sugarless cereals sweetened with fresh or dried fruit, maple syrup or molasses; granola, muesli	SUGAR COOKIES	Cookies sweetened with fruit juice concentrate or other natural sweeteners
		HIGH-SUGAR CAKES	Cakes made with natural sweeteners, natural angel food cake

Rise & Shine!

Rise & Shine!

There's simply no substitute for a good breakfast. At no other time of the day does the axiom "You are what you eat" hold so true. The foods we eat in the morning influence how we think and feel the rest of the day. A steaming bowl of oatmeal, a stack of whole-grain pancakes or a warm muffin spread with fruit preserves fuels the body for the hectic day ahead.

It wasn't so long ago that Americans believed a healthy breakfast included a couple of eggs sunnyside-up and a few slices of bacon. Over the last decade, however, nutrition researchers have shown us that this kind of breakfast is high in saturated fats, cholesterol and chemical additives; in short, it's hazardous to our health.

Instead, we should be eating fruits and whole grains, foods brimming with essential nutrients such as vitamins A and C, complex carbohydrates and fiber. If this sounds boring, think again. Once you've tried our *Delicious!* Cranberry Pecan Waffles With Pineapple-Orange Topping (page 26) or our Blue Horizon Fruit Cakes (page 29), you'll discover how easy it is to whip up a spectacular, nourishing breakfast.

If you tend to skip breakfast because you can't seem to get moving in the morning, follow these shortcuts:

- Natural, multi-grain pancake and waffle mixes require nothing more than the addition of water and can be whipped up in seconds. Flavor them with anything from chopped nuts to grated orange rind.

- Make it even easier on yourself! Freeze cooked pancakes and waffles, then thaw in the toaster oven or microwave for super-fast breakfasts.

- For fresh-baked muffins, mix wet ingredients (milk, oil, eggs, water) in one bowl and dry (flour, baking soda, salt) in another. Cover, place in the refrigerator overnight, combine and bake the next morning.

Eggless Country Scramble

Serves 4

Prep Time: 5 minutes
Cooking Time: 15 minutes

1	pound regular tofu, drained and crumbled
2	tablespoons tamari
1	tablespoon nutritional yeast
½	cup chopped onion
2	red potatoes, diced
½	cup sliced fresh mushrooms
½	cup chopped green bell pepper
1	clove garlic, minced
½	teaspoon thyme
½	teaspoon caraway seeds
½	teaspoon red pepper flakes
1	tomato, cut in wedges for garnish

Cholesterol-free tofu stands in for eggs in this savory classic. Serve with Herbed Biscuit Twists (page 47) and Tomato Marimba (page 228) for a hearty, low-fat weekend brunch.

1. In a small bowl, blend tofu with tamari and yeast and set aside.

2. Heat oil in a large, nonstick skillet over medium heat. Sauté onions and potatoes about 5 minutes until onions are translucent and potatoes are golden-brown. Add mushrooms, green pepper, garlic and spices and cook 3 to 5 minutes longer until peppers and mushrooms are soft. Transfer vegetables to a bowl.

3. Return skillet to low heat and sauté tofu until dry, about 3 minutes. Add vegetables to tofu, scramble well and cook just until vegetables are heated through.

4. Serve immediately with wedges of fresh tomato.

Calories per serving:	255
Grams of fat:	8.7
Percentage fat calories:	30%
Cholesterol:	0 mg.

Granola Baked Pears With Fruit Glaze

Serves 2

Prep Time: 10 minutes
Baking Time: 12 minutes

¼   cup blueberry or other flavor fruit syrup

6   tablespoons orange juice

2   tablespoons granola

2   ripe pears, peeled and cored

A warm piece of baked fruit cradling a juicy tumble of granola makes a terrific breakfast and a unique way to enjoy your orange juice, cereal and fruit. If you have a microwave oven, this recipe can be prepared in less than the 12 minutes specified. If not, it will cook to perfection while you're brewing herbal tea and doing a few morning stretches.

1. Preheat broiler. Combine syrup and half the orange juice in a small saucepan. Bring to a simmer, stirring occasionally, and cook 5 minutes. Combine granola with remaining orange juice.

2. Cut pears in half crosswise. Place in a shallow baking dish and broil 5 minutes or just until the edges begin to brown.

3. Remove from oven. Divide granola mixture evenly among pears to fill them and broil another 5 minutes until crisped. Pour warm syrup over pears.

Calories per serving:	*164*
Grams of fat:	*3.6*
Percentage fat calories:	*12%*
Cholesterol:	*0 mg.*

Bubbling Blueberry Bake

Serves 8

Prep Time: 10 minutes
Cooking Time: 20 minutes

4	cups frozen blueberries
⅔	cup date sugar
1	teaspoon grated orange peel
	Juice from one orange
2	teaspoons arrowroot
1	tablespoon cold water
2	egg whites
¼	teaspoon cream of tartar
2	cups muesli

Use organic frozen berries and drizzle with kefir for an added treat.

1. Preheat oven to 350°F. Combine blueberries with ⅓ cup date sugar, orange peel and juice in a saucepan. Stir cold water into arrowroot, add to blueberries and bring to a boil. Remove from heat.

2. Beat egg whites until fluffy. Add cream of tartar and continue to beat until stiff peaks form. Beat in remaining date sugar. Fold in muesli.

3. Put ⅓ of muesli mixture in the bottom of a 2-quart baking dish. Add blueberry mixture and top with remaining muesli. Bake until lightly browned and bubbling hot, about 20 minutes.

Calories per serving:	*189*
Grams of fat:	*1.3*
Percentage fat calories:	*6%*
Cholesterol:	*0 mg.*

Grape/Nut Couscous Breakfast Salad

Serves 4 to 6

Prep Time: 5 minutes
Cooking Time: 5 minutes

1   12-ounce package whole wheat couscous (about 4 cups cooked)

¼   cup lemonade

½   cup red and green grapes

½   cup toasted pecans or walnuts

Here's a fast and tasty alternative to cereal that can be enjoyed warm or at room temperature, plain or dolloped with yogurt, at any time of day. Quick-cooking whole wheat couscous — a good source of fiber — makes this ideal for busy mornings. For a heartier breakfast, toss in chunks of cooked turkey sausage.

1.   Prepare couscous according to package directions. Place in a medium bowl and drizzle with lemonade, tossing well.

2.   Gently stir in grapes and pecans, tossing again. Serve plain or topped with yogurt.

Note: *To reduce fat in this recipe, use ¼ cup nuts.*

Calories per serving:	*209*
Grams of fat:	*8.4*
Percentage fat calories:	*36%*
Cholesterol:	*0 mg.*

Banana Raisin Oat Bran Waffles

Yields 4 waffles

Prep Time: 5 minutes
Cooking Time: 6 minutes each

1   cup oat bran pancake and waffle mix (or make your own mix*)

½   teaspoon cinnamon

1   cup water

½   cup seedless raisins

1   banana, mashed

*Multi-Grain Pancake & Waffle Mix

Blend together:

1¼ cups whole wheat flour

1¼ cups unbleached white flour

½   cup corn flour or cornmeal

½   cup oat flour or rolled oats

¼   cup buckwheat flour

4   teaspoons baking powder

1½ teaspoons baking soda

½   teaspoon sea salt

¼   cup nonfat dry milk

This recipe yields 4 cups of multi-grain pancake and waffle mix.

Try these hearty waffles on a frosty winter morning. Serve with pure maple syrup, juice-sweetened fruit syrup or natural fruit preserves. Dried apricots and dates or fresh strawberries, kiwi, pineapple, melon and berries make pleasing garnishes.

1. Preheat waffle iron, pancake griddle or large nonstick skillet. Place waffle mix and cinnamon in a medium bowl and quickly stir in water with a fork, then fold in raisins and banana.

2. Ladle by half-cups onto the preheated iron or griddle and bake 4 to 6 minutes until golden and crisp around the edges.

Note: For more successful waffle making, brush the iron lightly with oil, even if it has a nonstick surface. Be sure the waffle iron is hot before pouring in the batter. Finally, remember that the browner the waffle, the crisper. If you prefer a chewier waffle, be sure to check periodically throughout the cooking time.

Calories per serving:	181
Grams of fat:	1.2
Percentage fat calories:	6%
Cholesterol:	0 mg.

Cranberry Pecan Waffles With Pineapple Orange Topping

Yields 4 waffles

Prep Time: 10 minutes
Cooking Time: 5 minutes each

1	cup whole-grain pancake and waffle mix (see our pancake mix recipe, page 25)
1	cup water
1	tablespoon vegetable oil
½	cup cranberries, chopped
½	cup toasted pecans, chopped
2	teaspoons orange zest
	Dash of ground cloves

Topping:

½	cup fruit-sweetened pineapple preserves
	Juice of 1 orange

You can quickly transform everyday whole-grain pancake and waffle mix into sublime waffles with a few simple additions. Just follow the package directions to prepare 3 to 4 waffles. If you like, prepare the waffles ahead of time and freeze until firm in a single layer on a cookie sheet. Then wrap in airtight plastic bags. To reheat, bake the frozen waffles in a preheated oven for 5 to 10 minutes or until hot.

1. Preheat waffle iron. Add water and oil to waffle mix and stir until just combined. Fold in cranberries, pecans, orange zest and cloves.

2. Pour ⅔ to ¾ cup batter into hot waffle iron and bake 3 to 5 minutes until lightly browned. Repeat with remaining batter. Serve with Pineapple Orange Topping.

3. To prepare topping, combine preserves and juice in a small saucepan and heat until warm.

Calories per serving:	*372*
Grams of fat:	*15*
Percentage fat calories:	*37%*
Cholesterol:	*0 mg.*

Raspberry Waffles With Cider Syrup

Yields 4 waffles

Prep Time: 15 minutes
Cooking Time: 20 minutes

1   cup whole-grain pancake
     and waffle mix (see our
     pancake mix recipe on
     page 25)

1   cup water

1   tablespoon vegetable oil

¼   cup chopped almonds

⅓   cup fresh raspberries or
     other fruit, well drained

3   cups unfiltered apple
     cider

These crowd-pleasing waffles become extraordinary when a handful of late-summer raspberries is tossed into the batter. Any fairly firm fruit such as apple, peach or pear chunks, or blueberries can be substituted with equally flavorful results. Look for new, natural syrups that combine fruit juice with pure maple syrup or try our suggestion for boiling down unfiltered apple cider until it's syrupy.

1. In a mixing bowl, combine waffle mix, water and oil, stirring until well-combined. (This step can be done the night before. Just cover and refrigerate, letting batter return to room temperature before proceeding with the recipe.) Stir in almonds and raspberries.

2. Preheat waffle iron and brush lightly with oil. Ladle waffle batter by half-cups onto the hot waffle iron and bake 4 to 6 minutes until golden and crisp around the edges. Keep in mind that it's best not to open the iron until the waffle stops steaming — this will help you avoid torn waffles. If desired, keep waffles warm in a 200°F oven.

3. Meanwhile, make syrup by gently boiling cider over moderate heat until it thickens to syrup consistency. To serve, drizzle over waffles.

Calories per serving:	206
Grams of fat:	6
Percentage fat calories:	26%
Cholesterol:	0 mg.

Morningside Blintzes

Serves 6 to 8

Prep Time: 15 minutes
Chilling Time: 1 hour
Cooking Time: 20 minutes

Crepes:

½ **cup whole wheat pastry flour**

¾ **cup nonfat dairy milk or 1% fat soy milk**

1½ **tablespoons vegetable oil**

1 **egg**

2 **egg whites**

Dash of sea salt

Filling:

1 **cake soft tofu, ½ pound, well drained**

3 **tablespoons fruit preserves**

½ **cup currants**

1½ **tablespoons grated orange rind**

If you only know blintzes as an extravagant brunch dish starring a sinfully sweet cheese filling, you're going to love these whole wheat alternatives. The creamy filling is tofu pureed with fruit preserves and sparked with currants and orange rind.

1. To make crepes, combine flour, milk, oil, egg, egg whites and salt in a blender or food processor and process until smooth. Chill batter for an hour.

2. Heat an 8-inch skillet or crepe pan until water dances on the surface, then oil lightly and make crepes one at a time, using 2 tablespoons of batter for each crepe. Cook each crepe on one side only. This will take just 2 to 3 minutes per crepe. Turn out cooked side up on a plate or clean kitchen towel. (The recipe can be prepared ahead to this point, and the crepes frozen between layers of waxed paper. To serve, thaw and warm in a toaster oven.)

3. To make filling, combine tofu and preserves in a blender or food processor and puree until smooth. Stir in currants and orange rind.

4. To serve, place 2 tablespoons of filling in each crepe and roll or fold. Drizzle with maple or fruit syrup.

Calories per serving:	177
Grams of fat:	6
Percentage fat calories:	30%
Cholesterol:	35.5 mg.

Blue Horizon Fruit Cakes

Serves 4

Prep Time: 10 minutes
Cooking Time: 15 minutes

1   **cup buckwheat pancake mix (see our pancake mix recipe on page 25)**

¾   **cup blue cornmeal**

1   **teaspoon baking powder**

1   **cup brewed blueberry or blackberry herbal tea**

¼   **cup nonfat dairy milk or 1% fat soy milk**

½   **cup blueberry preserves**

     Fresh strawberries for garnish

Blue cornmeal adds interest — plus potassium, iron and protein — to these naturally sweetened flapjacks. Buckwheat pancake mix provides the base, and brewed berry tea contributes a flavorful dimension.

1. In a mixing bowl, combine pancake mix, cornmeal and baking powder. Gradually stir in tea and milk.

2. Gently fold in blueberry preserves. Drop by ¼-cup measure onto a hot, lightly greased griddle or skillet. Turn once when bubbles appear on the surface of the pancake. Garnish with strawberries.

Calories per serving:	352
Grams of fat:	3.3
Percentage fat calories:	8%
Cholesterol:	0 mg.

Heavenly Quinoa Hash

Serves 6

Prep Time: 5 minutes
Cooking Time: 20 minutes

1	cup raw quinoa
2	cups water
¼	teaspoon sea salt
2	cooked potatoes, diced
1	onion, sliced
2	cloves garlic, minced
1	green or red bell pepper, diced
¼	cup minced parsley
	Salt-free herb blend to taste
1	tablespoon vegetable oil

A perfect way to use leftovers! Flavor quinoa and potatoes with your favorite spice blend for a powerful, protein-rich way to start your day.

1. Rinse quinoa under running water for several minutes. Bring water and salt to a boil. Stir in quinoa, cover and simmer 15 minutes until grains become translucent and pop open. Drain immediately.

2. Combine quinoa with remaining ingredients except oil. Taste and adjust seasonings.

3. Sauté hash in oil until warmed thoroughly and lightly browned.

Calories per serving:	*327*
Grams of fat:	*6.7*
Percentage fat calories:	*19%*
Cholesterol:	*0 mg.*

Fluffy Asparagus Tofu Quiche

Serves 10

Prep Time: 20 minutes
Cooking Time: 30 minutes

1	frozen whole wheat pie shell
1	cup diced onion
1	tablespoon minced garlic
2	teaspoons vegetable oil
1	pound asparagus, steamed and diced
3	tablespoons tarragon, minced
¾	pound silken tofu
⅛	teaspoon turmeric
2	tablespoons water
	Sea salt and black pepper to taste

Use tofu for a savory filling that will wow your family without the usual cream and eggs found in a quiche.

1. Preheat oven to 375°F. Sauté onion and garlic in oil until wilted. Remove from heat and stir in asparagus and tarragon.

2. In a food processor or blender, puree tofu with turmeric, water, salt and pepper until smooth. Combine with asparagus mixture. Taste and adjust seasonings.

3. Pour into pie shell and bake in center of oven until custard is set, about 30 minutes. Serve warm.

Calories per serving:	*128*
Grams of fat:	*7*
Percentage fat calories:	*49%*
Cholesterol:	*0 mg.*

Bagel & Smoked Salmon With Pimiento Deli Spread

Serves 4

Prep Time: 15 minutes

- ¾   **pound soft tofu, drained and crumbled**
- 1   **tablespoon vegetable oil**
- 1   **tablespoon apple cider vinegar**
- ½   **teaspoon honey**
     Freshly ground black pepper
- 2   **tablespoons sweet pickle relish**
- ¼   **cup chopped pimientos**
- 4   **whole wheat bagels, halved**
- 1   **pound sliced smoked salmon**
     Dill sprigs and lemon wedges for garnish

Smoked salmon with plenty of cream cheese makes a sublime bagel topping, but it's off limits to those monitoring their consumption of dietary fat. This simple spread will win instant fans, and the fact that it's made with tofu means it's great for low-cholesterol diets. The taste is nothing short of fabulous.

1. In a blender or food processor, combine half the tofu, the oil, vinegar, honey and pepper. Puree until smooth, then scrape into a medium bowl.

2. Stir in remaining tofu, relish and pimientos, then cover and refrigerate for an hour if possible.

3. To serve, toast the bagels and spread generously with the tofu mixture. Top with slices of salmon and garnish with lemon slices and parsley.

Calories per serving:	*482*
Grams of fat:	*12*
Percentage fat calories:	*23%*
Cholesterol:	*26 mg.*

Oven-Fresh & Fabulous Quick Breads

The wholesome aroma of our *Delicious!* whole-grain muffins, savory biscuits or fruit-sweetened bread baking in the oven will fill your household with a sense of well-being. Family and friends will think you labored hours in the kitchen when you serve them a basket of warm, pineapple-filled Piña Colada Muffins (page 42) or Herbed Biscuit Twists (page 47). The truth is, it will take you less than 10 minutes to stir up any one of our quick bread recipes.

We've adapted ready-made whole-grain baking mixes, available at your natural foods store, to take the effort out of creating healthful, heartwarming breads. Natural baking mixes eliminate several steps in the preparation process and, since there's little or no measuring of dry ingredients, cleanup is minimal. *(If you don't have whole-grain baking mix on hand, use this formula to blend your own: 2 cups whole wheat pastry flour, 1½ teaspoons aluminum-free baking powder, ¼ cup dried nonfat milk, and ⅛ teaspoon salt.)*

For muffins with made-from-scratch flavor and texture, mix up a batch of low-fat *Delicious!* Basic Muffins (page 36) and fold in your favorite ingredients. This versatile recipe makes it easy for you to invent your own sensational creations.

An excellent source of dietary fiber as well as complex carbohydrates, protein, minerals and B vitamins, whole-grain breads pack nutritional power. A couple of our Pear And Oat Bran Scones (page 43) will fortify you for a full morning of work or fun.

Once you've tried our jiffy Lemon Yogurt Tea Muffins (page 41) or our Raspberry Coffeecake Bran Muffins (page 40), you'll be inspired to try a different recipe every day. Family and friends will feel so nurtured by your labor of love. Only you have to know how little effort went into making these gems.

Why Soy Milk?

We specify nonfat dairy milk or 1% fat soy milk instead of whole milk in our bread recipes to reduce fat and cholesterol. If you haven't already discovered it, soy milk is an excellent substitute for dairy milk in baked goods as well as beverages, desserts, soups and entrees. Measure for measure, soy milk contains more protein, iron and B vitamins than dairy milk but less fat, fewer calories and no cholesterol. The table below compares the fat and cholesterol composition of dairy milk and soy milk.

Soy Milk vs. Dairy Milk

For people who are allergic to cow's milk or wish to cut dairy products from their diet to lower their cholesterol and saturated fat intakes, soy milk is a delicious, healthy alternative.

	Calories	Fat	Saturated Fat	Cholesterol
Whole dairy milk, 1 cup	159	8.5 gm	4.7 gm	30 mg
Nonfat or skim dairy milk, 1 cup	88	.4 gm	.3 gm	4 mg
Soy milk, 1 cup	127	5.0 gm	.4 gm	0 mg
1% fat soy milk, 1 cup	100	2.0 gm	.4 gm	0 mg

Egg Replacer

Most of our quick bread recipes call for egg whites and, in some cases, whole eggs. However, you can substitute fat-free, cholesterol-free "egg replacer" for eggs, if desired. Egg replacer, which is made from potato starch and tapioca, is available in natural foods stores. Or you can make your own using this recipe: **Combine 1 teaspoon arrowroot powder, 1 teaspoon soy flour and a pinch of lecithin with ½ cup warm water. Use as a substitute for 2 eggs in any recipe.**

Delicious! Basic Muffins

Yields 10 to 12 muffins

Prep Time: 10 to 15 minutes
Baking Time: 20 minutes

1½   **cups unbleached white flour**

1½   **cups whole wheat flour or 1½ cups whole wheat pastry flour**

4   **teaspoons baking powder**

1   **teaspoon sea salt**

4   **egg whites**

⅓   **cup honey (½ cup for sweeter muffins)**

½   **cup nonfat dairy milk or 1% fat soy milk**

½   **cup nonfat plain yogurt**

¼   **cup vegetable oil**

Use this muffin recipe to make Fresh Strawberry Orange Muffins (page 37) and Lemon Poppy Seed Muffins (page 38) – or create your own variation.

1. Preheat oven to 400°F. In a mixing bowl, sift together all dry ingredients.

2. In another bowl, beat egg whites until frothy and stir in honey, milk, yogurt and oil. Pour egg white mixture over dry ingredients and fold in until just combined. Do not overmix.

3. Scoop batter into well-greased or paper-lined muffin cups. (Use an ice cream scoop for smoother and more accurate measuring.) For large muffins, fill cups completely with batter.

4. Bake 20 minutes or until muffins are lightly browned and a knife or toothpick slides out easily. Turn out on a rack to cool.

Calories per serving:	185
Grams of fat:	5
Percentage fat calories:	24%
Cholesterol:	0 mg.

Fresh Strawberry Orange Muffins

Yields 10 to 12 muffins

Prep Time: 10 to 15 minutes
Baking Time: 20 minutes

Ingredients for Basic Muffins (page 36)

Zest of one orange, or to taste

1½ **cups strawberries, quartered**

These beautiful muffins are almost like miniature strawberry shortcakes. Serve warm with a spoonful of yogurt or whipped cream for an easy spring dessert.

1. Follow directions for Basic Muffins (page 36).

2. Add orange zest to wet ingredients before stirring into dry ingredients. Fold in strawberries at the end. To prevent strawberries from juicing, be sure there is still a little bit of flour in the batter to coat them. Bake as directed.

Calories per serving:	191
Grams of fat:	5.2
Percentage fat calories:	24%
Cholesterol:	0 mg.

Lemon Poppy Seed Muffins

Yields 10 to 12 muffins

Prep Time: 10 to 15 minutes
Baking Time: 20 minutes

Ingredients for Basic Muffins (page 36)

3 tablespoons poppy seeds

Zest of 1 lemon

Juice from 1 lemon

Perfect for breakfast, tea or snack time, aromatic Lemon Poppy Seed Muffins are complemented by a spread of equal portions of cream cheese and orange marmalade.

1. Follow directions for Basic Muffins (page 36).

2. Add poppy seeds to dry ingredients and add lemon zest and juice to wet ingredients before combining. Bake as directed.

Calories per serving:	197
Grams of fat:	6
Percentage fat calories:	27%
Cholesterol:	0 mg.

Apple Carrot Gems

Yields 12 muffins

Prep Time: 15 minutes
Baking Time: 20 minutes

1 tablespoon sesame seeds

1¾ cups whole wheat pastry
flour

2 teaspoons baking powder

1½ teaspoons baking blend
spice (or ½ teaspoon
each cinnamon, nutmeg
and allspice)

⅛ teaspoon sea salt

¾ cup grated carrot

¼ cup chopped dates

3 egg whites

¼ cup maple syrup

1 cup applesauce

¼ cup vegetable oil

¼ cup apple juice

*These dense, nourishing muffins are moist and very
filling. You can substitute natural carrot cake mix if you're in
a hurry. In either case, refrigerate a week's worth and freeze
the extra muffins to reheat in a slow oven on some rainy, lazy
morning.*

1. Preheat oven to 400°F. Lightly oil a twelve-muffin
pan and sprinkle with sesame seeds.

2. In a mixing bowl, combine flour, baking powder,
spices and salt. Stir in carrots and dates, tossing to
coat well.

3. Place egg whites in another bowl and beat until
frothy. Stir in syrup, applesauce, oil and juice and
mix well.

4. Add egg white mixture to dry ingredients and stir
just until combined. Divide batter evenly among
muffin tins. Bake until tops are puffed, about 20
minutes.

Calories per serving:	174
Grams of fat:	5.7
Percentage fat calories:	30%
Cholesterol:	0 mg.

Raspberry Coffeecake Bran Muffins

Yields 12 muffins

Prep Time: 20 minutes
Baking Time: 25 to 30 minutes

Muffins:

2	tablespoons vegetable oil
¼	cup honey or molasses
2	egg whites, lightly beaten
1	cup water
1	10-ounce package bran muffin mix
1	cup raspberry preserves

Topping:

½	cup chopped nuts
½	cup maple granules or date sugar
¼	cup whole wheat pastry flour
1	teaspoon cinnamon
1	teaspoon grated lemon rind
2	tablespoons melted soy margarine, cooled

These ultra-rich muffins get their great taste from naturally sweet raspberry preserves. The crumbly streusel topping transforms them from ordinary muffins into miniature coffeecakes, ideal for brunch or an afternoon tea break with a friend.

1. Preheat oven to 350°F. In a large bowl, beat together oil, honey, egg whites and water. Stir in muffin mix until incorporated, then fold in raspberry preserves. Spoon batter into greased muffin tins.

2. In a small bowl, combine topping ingredients (mixture may be crumbly, but that's okay). Sprinkle over muffins. Bake 25 to 30 minutes until a toothpick inserted in the center comes out clean.

Calories per serving:	*257*
Grams of fat:	*7.6*
Percentage fat calories:	*27%*
Cholesterol:	*0 mg.*

Lemon Yogurt Tea Muffins

Yields 12 muffins

Prep Time: 10 minutes
Baking Time: 15 to 20 minutes

1½ cups whole-grain baking mix (or use the baking mix formula on page 34)

½ cup maple granules or granulated cane juice

¼ cup melted soy margarine or vegetable oil

2 egg whites, lightly beaten

½ cup brewed hibiscus herbal tea

2 tablespoons nonfat plain yogurt

1 tablespoon grated lemon peel

When baked in miniature muffin tins, these lemony muffins make delectable little tea sandwiches. Try them with a filling of apricot jam, orange marmalade or other pure fruit preserve and a sprinkling of slivered almonds.

1. Preheat oven to 325°F. Coat a muffin tin lightly with vegetable oil.

2. In a mixing bowl, combine all ingredients, taking care not to overmix.

3. Fill muffin cups ¾ full and bake 15 to 20 minutes until slightly golden around the edges.

Calories per serving:	*116*
Grams of fat:	*4*
Percentage fat calories:	*31%*
Cholesterol:	*0 mg.*

Piña Colada Muffins

Yields 8 muffins

Prep Time: 10 minutes
Baking Time: 20 minutes

1½ cups whole-grain baking
      mix (or use the baking
      mix formula on page 34)

2   teaspoons baking powder

½   cup oat bran

¼   cup flaked coconut

¼   cup vegetable oil

2   egg whites, lightly beaten

1   cup piña colada (coconut-
      pineapple) juice

½   cup nonfat dairy milk or
      1% fat soy milk

1   cup pineapple chunks

Here's a taste of the tropics in a muffin that's tender, fruity and rich tasting.

1. Preheat oven to 375°F. In a mixing bowl, combine baking mix, baking powder, oat bran and coconut.

2. Stir in oil, egg whites, piña colada juice and milk. Gently fold in pineapple chunks. Spoon batter into lightly greased muffin tins.

3. Bake for 20 minutes or until a toothpick inserted in the center comes out clean. Turn out onto a rack to cool.

Calories per serving:	217
Grams of fat:	9
Percentage fat calories:	37%
Cholesterol:	0 mg.

Pear & Oat Bran Scones

Yields 8 scones

Prep Time: 20 minutes
Baking Time: 10 to 20 minutes

1   cup whole-grain baking mix (or use the baking mix formula on page 34)

1   teaspoon cinnamon

⅓   cup soy margarine

1   cup oat bran cereal or oatmeal

⅓   cup chopped raisins

¾   cup chopped pear

2   egg whites, lightly beaten

2   tablespoons apple juice

2   tablespoons honey

1   teaspoon vanilla

We've eliminated the cholesterol-rich egg yolk in these tasty, quick bread treats. Best when served warm from the oven, these scones are delicious with a dab of natural fruit preserves to enhance the juicy pear flavor.

1. Preheat oven to 400°F. In a small mixing bowl, combine baking mix and cinnamon. Cut in margarine until mixture resembles coarse crumbs.

2. Stir in oat bran cereal, raisins and pear. Add egg whites, apple juice, honey and vanilla and mix well. The dough may be a bit sticky.

3. Use a nonstick baking sheet or coat a regular one lightly with oil. With floured hands, divide dough into eight balls, place on baking sheet and flatten slightly.

4. Brush tops with a little honey. Bake 10 to 20 minutes until golden around the edges.

Calories per serving:	*216*
Grams of fat:	*8.5*
Percentage fat calories:	*35%*
Cholesterol:	*0 mg.*

Lemony Banana Nut Bread

Yields 1 loaf (12 slices)

Prep Time: 10 minutes
Baking Time: 30 to 40 minutes

1   very ripe banana

2   egg whites, lightly beaten

2   cups whole-grain baking
     mix (or use the baking
     mix formula on page 34)

¾   cup honey (reserve
     ¼ cup for glaze)

½   cup nonfat plain yogurt

½   cup pecans (optional)

     Juice of 1 lemon

A lemony glaze and crunchy pecans give this easy quick bread pizazz.

1. Preheat oven to 350°F. In a large bowl, beat banana and egg whites with a hand mixer until smooth. Add baking mix, ½ cup honey, yogurt and pecans and mix until just combined.

2. Pour batter into a greased loaf pan and bake 30 to 40 minutes until a toothpick slides out easily when inserted.

3. Combine lemon juice and reserved honey and drizzle over the warm bread. Cool thoroughly before removing from the pan.

Calories per serving:	186
Grams of fat:	4
Percentage fat calories:	19%
Cholesterol:	0 mg.

Cranberry Walnut Bread

Yields 1 loaf (12 slices)

Prep Time: 30 minutes
Baking Time: 1 hour

2½ cups whole wheat pastry flour

1 teaspoon baking powder

½ teaspoon baking soda

½ teaspoon sea salt

1 cup soft tofu

1 cup pineapple-orange juice concentrate

½ cup honey

1 teaspoon vanilla extract

1 cup ripe bananas, mashed

2 egg whites

1½ cups fresh cranberries

1 tablespoon finely grated orange rind

1 cup walnuts, large pieces

Serve this tasty nondairy bread for dessert with organic coffee or tea.

1. Preheat oven to 350°F. In a large bowl, combine flour, baking powder, baking soda and salt.

2. In a food processor, cream tofu, juice, honey, vanilla, egg whites and bananas.

3. Stir the creamed tofu mixture into the flour mixture and mix well with a large wooden spoon.

4. Fold in the cranberries, orange rind and nuts.

5. Pour batter into an oiled loaf pan and bake 1 hour until a toothpick inserted into the bread's center comes out clean.

6. Cool 30 minutes before removing from pan.

Calories per serving:	*305*
Grams of fat:	*7.5*
Percentage fat calories:	*22%*
Cholesterol:	*0 mg.*

Orange Pine Nut Tea Ring

Serves 6 to 8

Prep Time: 10 minutes
Baking Time: 25 to 30 minutes

1   6-ounce package carrot
    cake mix

2   egg whites, lightly beaten

1   8-ounce container lemon
    or vanilla low-fat yogurt

¼   cup pine nuts

¼   cup orange juice

3   tablespoons maple syrup,
    maple granules or gran-
    ulated cane juice

1   large orange, halved and
    thinly sliced

¼   cup fresh or defrosted
    frozen cranberries

Make tea time or dessert time a real treat with this quick bread delightfully decorated with a rainbow of fruit.

1. Preheat oven to 350°F. In a mixing bowl, combine cake mix, egg whites, yogurt, 1 tablespoon pine nuts and orange juice.

2. Lightly oil a ring-shaped cake pan. You can also use a loaf or round pan. Distribute maple syrup or other sweetener evenly around bottom of pan and arrange orange slices, cranberries and remaining pine nuts in an interesting pattern over sweetener.

3. Carefully spoon cake batter over fruit and nuts, smoothing top surface. Bake 25 to 30 minutes until a toothpick inserted in the center comes out clean. Let cool slightly, then invert onto a plate to cool completely.

Calories per serving:	161
Grams of fat:	3.3
Percentage fat calories:	18%
Cholesterol:	1.3 mg.

Herbed Biscuit Twists

Yields 12 biscuits

Prep Time: 15 minutes
Baking Time: 12 to 15 minutes

1	recipe whole-grain biscuit mix, prepared according to package directions
2	tablespoons minced fresh herbs such as dill, tarragon or parsley, or 2 teaspoons dried
1	egg white, beaten
3	tablespoons sesame seeds

Natural packaged biscuit mix makes a wonderfully versatile dough, especially when combined with fresh or dried herbs and formed into festive-looking twists. You can also try making miniature braided breadsticks by intertwining three strips of dough, then baking as directed.

1. Preheat oven to 350°F. On a lightly floured surface, briefly knead minced herbs into the biscuit dough. Roll out dough to ¼-inch thickness. With a knife, cut out strips of dough about 5 inches long and 2 inches wide.

2. Twist each strip loosely to form a spiral and place on a lightly greased cookie sheet. Brush each twist with beaten egg white and sprinkle with the sesame seeds. Bake 12 to 15 minutes until golden and slightly crisp.

Calories per serving:	*122*
Grams of fat:	*2.7*
Percentage fat calories:	*20%*
Cholesterol:	*0 mg.*

Blue Bayou Corn Sticks

Yields 18 corn sticks

Prep Time: 10 minutes
Baking Time: 25 minutes

1   cup blue cornmeal

2   cups whole wheat pastry
     flour

⅛   teaspoon sea salt

4   teaspoons baking powder

1   cup nonfat dairy milk or
     1% fat soy milk

¼   cup vegetable oil or
     melted soy margarine

¼   cup barley or rice malt
     syrup

2   eggs, beaten

½   cup fresh or frozen corn
     kernels (optional – you
     could substitute chopped
     bell pepper or 1 table-
     spoon chopped jalapeños
     for corn)

Chances are, you've come across blue cornmeal in your local natural foods store — in the form of corn chips, pancake mix, taco shells or just plain meal. It makes a distinctive, purplish corn stick (or muffin, if you can't find a cast-iron corn stick pan) that tastes sensational and is sure to stimulate conversation among your guests.

1. Preheat oven to 400°F. In a medium bowl, whisk milk, oil or margarine, malt syrup and eggs to combine.

2. In a mixing bowl, combine cornmeal, flour, salt and baking powder. Make a well in the center and add milk mixture, stirring as briefly as possible. Gently fold in corn.

3. Spoon batter into two lightly greased corn stick or muffin pans. Bake 12 to 15 minutes or until a toothpick inserted in the center comes out clean. Turn out onto a rack to cool.

Calories per serving:	*151*
Grams of fat:	*4.6*
Percentage fat calories:	*28%*
Cholesterol:	*24 mg.*

Party Time!

Party Time!

Parties are a wonderful chance for friends to gather and share an intimate evening. They're even more fun when they're easy for the host.

Here, we've collected tempting appetizers that will leave you time to enjoy the festivities. You'll love such easy, taste-tempting treats as Falafel-Hummus Tartlets (page 64) and Steamed Umeboshi Rice Balls (page 67). In the interest of a low-fat diet, we've incorporated tips on substituting ingredients. For example, use low-fat mozzarella instead of feta cheese in our Red Roasted Peppers (page 65).

To make party planning a cinch, follow these simple guidelines:

- Plan the menu at least one month before the party to allow time for testing recipes.

- Remember, guests appreciate hors d'oeuvres that are easy to pick up with their fingers. Avoid drippy sauces and foods that require a knife and fork.

- Use our tried-and-true formula for a tantalizing appetizer buffet: Serve one dip with crudités or chips, one spread (pâté or mousse) with crackers, mini-muffins, or French bread rounds, and three hors d'oeuvres (finger foods). You may also want to serve a dessert, depending on the occasion and time of day.

- Choose a combination of appetizers with contrasting yet complementary flavors, textures and colors such as Smoky Lentil Pâté; Scarlet Crudité Dip; Polenta, Spinach & Chevre Wedges; Basil Parmesan Bites and East Indian Cheewra.

- Select foods of varying degrees of difficulty to prepare; most should be very easy to make, leaving time for more complicated appetizers. Dips and spreads, which taste best when their flavors mingle, can be prepared a day in advance.

- When calculating how much food to prepare, figure each guest will eat 2 to 3 servings of one appetizer. Except for baked goods, most recipes can be doubled or tripled easily; however, you may need to adjust seasonings. If in doubt, test recipes first.

- Plan garnishes beforehand and add them to your shopping list. Avoid last-minute decisions.

East Indian Cheewra

Serves 15

Prep Time: 20 minutes
Cooking Time: 30 minutes

1 tablespoon sea salt

1 teaspoon black mustard seed (optional)

1 teaspoon curry powder

½ teaspoon garlic powder

¼ teaspoon cayenne pepper

¼ teaspoon nutmeg

¼ teaspoon black pepper

¼ teaspoon cloves

¼ teaspoon cinnamon

½ cup raw pumpkin seeds

½ cup raw whole almonds

½ cup raw whole peanuts

½ cup raw whole cashews

½ cup raw whole walnuts

½ cup golden raisins

2 cups puffed dry cereal

2 tablespoons vegetable oil

2 tablespoons honey

Cheewra is a spicy, curried nut and grain party mix. It contains just a hint of hot, and the spiced nuts produce an intriguing flavor.

1. Heat oven to 325°F.

2. Mix spices in a small bowl.

3. Mix nuts, seeds and cereal in a separate bowl.

4. Heat oil in a skillet and add spices. Stir constantly until spices are lightly roasted. Add honey and heat until bubbly.

5. Add nut and cereal mixture to hot spices and mix well, coating nuts.

6. Spread evenly on a cookie sheet and bake 25 to 30 minutes until golden brown. Stir occasionally.

7. Allow nuts to cool before removing from cookie sheet. Add raisins and serve.

Note: *To reduce fat calories to 45 percent, replace almonds, peanuts and walnuts with 1½ cups of chestnuts, the lowest fat nut.*

Calories per serving:	185
Grams of fat:	14
Percentage fat calories:	69%
Cholesterol:	0 mg.

Smoky Lentil Pâté

Yields 4 cups

Prep Time: 20 minutes
Cooking Time: 10 minutes

2   cups cooked lentils

1   large carrot, steamed and
     coarsely chopped

2   tablespoons tamari

1   tablespoon smoked
     nutritional yeast

1   teaspoon minced onion

2   tablespoons arrowroot

1   tablespoon minced fresh
     parsley

This pâté is a power-packed blend of quick-cooking legumes, carrots and flavored yeast — a perfect spread for whole-grain crackers.

1. In a blender or food processor, combine lentils and carrot with slightly less than 1 cup water and puree until smooth. Add tamari, yeast and onion and puree to combine. Scrape into a small saucepan and warm over low heat, stirring frequently.

2. In a small bowl, dissolve arrowroot in 2 tablespoons cold water. Add to lentils and cook over moderate heat, stirring constantly until thickened, about 5 minutes. Remove from heat and stir in parsley. Pack into a crock, cover and refrigerate.

Calories per tablespoon:	*12*
Grams of fat:	*.04*
Percentage fat calories:	*3%*
Cholesterol:	*0 mg.*

Simply Stunning White Bean Pâté

Serves 6 to 8

Prep Time: 10 to 15 minutes
Cooking Time: 40 to 50 minutes

3	cups cooked white beans
½	cup parsley
3	green onions, chopped
10	whole wheat crackers
2	egg whites
½	cup nonfat dairy milk or 1% fat soy milk
¾	cup finely grated carrots
½	cup minced onion
3	garlic cloves, minced
	Sea salt and freshly ground black pepper to taste
2	teaspoons Italian herb blend
½	teaspoon cayenne pepper
1	red bell pepper, seeded and sliced lengthwise
½	pound asparagus, lightly steamed

Although a layered vegetable pâté is normally time-consuming to prepare, bottled natural white beans and a food processor cut down the preparation time considerably. Omit the vegetable layers to trim more time.

1. Process beans, parsley, green onions, crackers, egg whites and milk in a blender or food processor until well combined.

2. In a large frying pan, sauté carrots, onion and garlic in ¼ cup water until soft, about 5 minutes.

3. Preheat oven to 400°F. In a large mixing bowl, combine bean mixture, sautéed vegetables and spices and stir well.

4. Place an oiled rectangle of waxed paper on the bottom of a greased loaf pan. Transfer ¼ of the pâté to pan and layer ½ of the red pepper on top. Repeat with more pâté, alternating with either asparagus or red pepper. Top with another piece of waxed paper, oiled side down. Bake 40 to 50 minutes or until firm.

5. Serve pâté warm or cold, either in the baking dish or turned out on a plate. Allow time for pâté to firm up before unmolding.

Calories per slice:	131
Grams of fat:	1.2
Percentage fat calories:	8%
Cholesterol:	0 mg.

Avocado Mousse

Serves 20

Prep Time: 30 minutes
Cooking Time: 5 minutes
Chilling Time: 4 hours

5	ripe avocadoes
¼	cup fresh lime juice
¼	cup salsa
3	tablespoons agar flakes, a sea vegetable substitute for gelatin
2	cups water
2	teaspoons sea salt

A feast for the eyes in addition to the palate, this creamy, nondairy concoction will bring rave reviews from your guests. Serve with crackers and colorful red pepper wedges.

1. Heat water in a small saucepan and stir in agar flakes. Bring to a boil, then lower heat and simmer 3 to 4 minutes until agar is completely dissolved. Set aside.

2. Slice avocadoes and combine with lime juice in a bowl.

3. Blend avocado, lime juice, salt and salsa in a food processor until velvety smooth.

4. Add agar solution and blend until completely smooth again.

5. Pour mixture into a nonstick 6-cup mold and chill for at least 4 hours in the refrigerator.

6. To unmold, set mold in hot water for 1 minute. Cover mold with a serving plate and invert. Shake firmly to loosen and lift mold away from mousse.

Note: *To reduce calories and fat, substitute 1½ cups of pureed split peas for two of the avocados called for in this recipe.*

Calories per serving:	*101*
Grams of fat:	*9*
Percentage fat calories:	*86%*
Cholesterol:	*0 mg.*

Scarlet Crudité Dip

Yields 2 cups

Prep Time: 5 minutes

1   pound soft tofu

1   red bell pepper, roasted, peeled, seeded and chopped (For how to roast red peppers, see Red Roasted Peppers, page 65.)

½   cup salsa

    Chopped fresh cilantro, for garnish

These days, a party just isn't complete without a display of crisp vegetables and something savory and smooth to accompany them. This quick dip takes just minutes to prepare, and it can be made up to 2 days in advance. Try it with corn or soy chips, too!

1. In a blender or food processor, combine tofu, pepper and salsa and process until pureed. Scrape into a serving bowl and stir just before serving. Garnish with cilantro.

Calories per tablespoon:	10
Grams of fat:	.5
Percentage fat calories:	43%
Cholesterol:	0 mg.

Vegemole

Yields 3 cups

Prep Time: 15 minutes

1   avocado, mashed

1   carrot, chopped

1   celery stalk, chopped

½   medium red bell pepper, chopped

1   cup nonfat plain yogurt

1   cup dill pickle relish or salsa

2   tablespoons chopped fresh cilantro

This chunky dip adds nonfat yogurt to an avocado to cut down on the fat content. Try it on a baked potato or grilled fish, too.

1. Combine all ingredients in a serving bowl and mix well.

Note: *This is oh so good with corn chips — blue corn, mixed-grain, unsalted, tamari-seasoned, you name it.*

Calories per tablespoon:	*10*
Grams of fat:	*.6*
Percentage fat calories:	*56%*
Cholesterol:	*0 mg.*

Jalapeño Cheese Spread

Yields 1 cup

Prep Time: 10 minutes

8   **ounces kefir cheese, softened**

2   **teaspoons granulated garlic**

3   **jalapeño peppers, minced**

½   **teaspoon sea salt**

¼   **cup chopped cilantro**

1   **red bell pepper, sliced**

4   **black olives, sliced**

Jalapeños and cilantro give this spread a lively Southwestern flair.

1. Combine cheese with garlic, jalapeños and salt. Mix well. Shape into a ball or other festive shape. Cover and chill one hour.

2. Coat cheese with cilantro and place on a bed of sliced red pepper. Garnish with black olives if desired and serve with corn chips or whole-grain crackers.

Note: *To reduce fat calories to 41%, substitute low-fat ricotta for kefir cheese.*

Calories per tablespoon:	37
Grams of fat:	3
Percentage fat calories:	75%
Cholesterol:	5 mg.

Mexican Pesto

Serves 15

Prep Time: 10 minutes

1   pound soft tofu

5   garlic cloves, peeled

1   jalapeño pepper, minced

1   bunch cilantro

2   tablespoons honey

2   tablespoons lemon juice

1   teaspoon sea salt

3   teaspoons ground cumin

½   pound jicama, sliced

1   red bell pepper, sliced

1   green bell pepper, sliced

This savory spread is perfect for a party dip or hors d'oeuvres.

1. Drain tofu thoroughly and set aside. Fit a food processor with metal chopping blade. With motor running, drop garlic and jalapeño into processor bowl and process until minced.

2. Remove and discard tough stems from cilantro. Process remaining cilantro leaves until finely minced. Add tofu and process one minute. Stir together honey and lemon juice to dissolve. Add to tofu mixture with salt and cumin. Process to blend.

3. Transfer spread to a serving bowl or store in an airtight container until ready to serve. If spread is made ahead, drain liquid from edges before serving. Serve with jicama and pepper slices for dipping.

Calories per serving:	*50*
Grams of fat:	*2*
Percentage fat calories:	*36%*
Cholesterol:	*0 mg.*

Layered Taos Bean Dip

Serves 6 to 8

Prep Time: 10 minutes

1 4.8-ounce package instant refried beans, prepared according to directions

½ cup nonfat plain yogurt

1 small zucchini, shredded and drained well on towels

½ Bermuda onion, chopped

6 pepperoncinis, chopped, or more to taste

4 ounces shredded cheese

1 cup shredded red leaf or other lettuce

½ yellow bell pepper, chopped

1 tomato, chopped

½ cup salsa

Tortilla chips

For ease of preparation, use a natural convenience mix that turns into spicy refried beans in less than 20 minutes. If you like more wild than mild, substitute jalapeños for the pepperoncinis (pickled Italian peppers).

1. Heat refried beans until bubbly and hot. In a round serving dish, layer ingredients in the order listed. Serve immediately with tortilla chips.

Calories per serving:	131
Grams of fat:	5
Percentage fat calories:	33%
Cholesterol:	12.5 mg.

One Potato, Sweet Potato Dip

Yields 3 cups

Prep Time: 10 minutes

- 1   cup, about 2 medium, cooked sweet potatoes
- 1   cup, about 2 medium, cooked carrots
- 1   cup nonfat plain yogurt
- 2   tablespoons mustard
- 1   teaspoon wasabi
- ¼ cup chopped toasted almonds

Enjoy this luscious puree with a handful of natural chips or other snacks (try rice cakes or oil-free Japanese rice crackers if you're really cutting fat), but be sure to include raw or lightly steamed vegetables as dippers, too. The recipe can also be used as a vegetable side dish to accompany fish or poultry.

1. Mash sweet potatoes and carrots together or puree in a blender or food processor in batches.

2. Scrape into a bowl and fold in yogurt, mustard, wasabi and nuts. Serve warm if desired with corn or mixed-grain chips.

Calories per tablespoon:	14
Grams of fat:	.4
Percentage fat calories:	28%
Cholesterol:	0 mg.

Apricot Glow

Yields 1½ cups

Prep Time: 10 minutes
Cooking Time: 15 minutes

1   cup unsweetened orange juice

½   cup chopped dried apricots or ½ cup apricot preserves

½   cup unsweetened applesauce

½   cup nonfat plain yogurt

     Dash of freshly ground nutmeg and ginger

Kids as well as grownups will favor this slightly sweet, slightly savory, mild yet intriguing dip. Try it with raw vegetables as well as with crunchy packaged snacks.

1. In a small saucepan, combine orange juice and apricots. (If using preserves, halve the amount of orange juice and skip the cooking step — just combine.) Bring to a boil, reduce heat to moderate and cook, stirring frequently, for 15 minutes or until apricots are soft and liquid is absorbed. Remove from heat.

2. When mixture has cooled, combine in a blender with applesauce and yogurt. Season to taste and chill until ready to serve.

Note: *This is especially delicious with plain, apple-cinnamon or honey-nut rice cakes, sesame crackers and amaranth or oat bran graham crackers.*

Calories per tablespoon:	18
Grams of fat:	0
Percentage fat calories:	0%
Cholesterol:	0 mg.

Basil-Parmesan Bites With Mellow Molasses Barbecue Dip

Yields 1½ dozen

Prep Time: 15 minutes
Cooking Time: 20 minutes

1   **4.4 ounce package tofu burger mix**

1   **10.5 ounce cake firm tofu, drained and mashed**

2   **tablespoons grated Parmesan cheese**

2   **tablespoons fresh basil, finely chopped**

Dip:

1   **tablespoon vegetable oil**

1   **large onion, chopped**

3   **garlic cloves, minced**

1   **cup catsup**

3   **tablespoons molasses**

1   **tablespoon grainy mustard**

¾   **cup unsweetened pineapple juice**

2   **teaspoons all-purpose herb blend**

These delectable little croquettes made with tofu burger mix and tofu are perfect spring party nibbles. We love them as a snack, speared with toothpicks and dunked in Mellow Molasses Barbecue Dip. They also work very nicely in a whole wheat croissant.

1.   Preheat oven to 325°F. In a medium bowl, combine tofu burger mix, tofu, cheese and basil. Roll into balls about 2 inches in diameter and place on an oiled baking sheet.

2.   Bake, turning once or twice, for 15 minutes or until golden. Keep warm until ready to serve.

3.   To prepare dipping sauce, sauté onion and garlic in vegetable oil over moderate heat 5 minutes until onion is transparent.

4.   Add remaining ingredients and blend well. Reduce heat to moderately low and simmer 15 minutes, stirring occasionally.

Calories per serving:	48
Grams of fat:	1.6
Percentage fat calories:	30%
Cholesterol:	0 mg.

Polenta, Spinach & Chevre Wedges

Serves 4

Prep Time: 20 minutes
Cooking Time: 15 minutes

2   cups water

⅔   cup corn grits or
     stoneground cornmeal

4   ounces goat cheese
     (chevre) or mozzarella,
     sliced

4   cups fresh spinach,
     washed and torn into
     bite-sized pieces

3   tablespoons Caesar salad
     dressing

2   tablespoons pine nuts

We used natural corn grits to make these tasty open-faced sandwiches, but coarsely ground cornmeal will do just as nicely. Once you've taken 10 minutes to cook the polenta, you can refrigerate it until ready to slice and grill or panfry these crunchy wedges. Incidentally, a few sliced shiitake mushrooms, cooked with the spinach, make this sandwich even more delicious.

1. In a medium saucepan, bring water to a boil. Stir in corn grits, cover and cook 5 minutes or until water has been absorbed. Stir well and spoon into a square or loaf pan. Let cool (refrigerate if desired) until firm enough to slice.

2. Preheat oven to 325°F. Cut polenta into triangles and place on a lightly greased baking pan. Bake 5 minutes, then turn and bake 5 minutes longer until the edges are crisp. Top with goat cheese.

3. While polenta bakes, steam spinach in the water that clings to it in a covered saucepan until it wilts slightly, about 5 minutes. Remove from heat, toss with salad dressing and pine nuts and set aside.

4. To serve, divide polenta wedges among 4 plates. Top with some of the spinach and enjoy.

Calories per serving:	262
Grams of fat:	26
Percentage fat calories:	89%
Cholesterol:	25 mg.

Falafel-Hummus Tartlets

Yields 2 dozen

Prep Time: 20 minutes
Cooking Time: 20 minutes

1   package falafel mix

1   cup hummus prepared
    from a mix

1   sun-dried tomato,
    slivered, for garnish

    Sprigs of parsley, for
    garnish

This remarkably simple recipe uses just two products, both available in natural mixes. The spicy flavor of the falafel is tempered by the filling of hummus (chickpea puree). You'll need a miniature muffin tin (or two), available in most department stores or houseware shops, to form the falafel cups. Or, you could just make minifalafel balls and serve with hummus for dipping.

1. Preheat oven to 350°F. Prepare falafel mix according to package directions. Press about 1 tablespoon in each cup of a well-oiled miniature muffin pan and bake 20 minutes until golden. Let cool and remove from pan. Repeat with remaining mix.

2. Shortly before serving, fill each falafel cup with ¾ tablespoon of hummus and garnish with parsley or sun-dried tomato.

Calories per piece:	*37*
Grams of fat:	*1.5*
Percentage fat calories:	*35%*
Cholesterol:	*0 mg.*

Red Roasted Peppers With Sun-Dried Tomato & Basil Dressing

Serves 10

Prep Time: 45 minutes
Cooking Time: 45 minutes

4   red bell peppers
1   pound feta cheese

Dressing:

¼   ounce sun-dried tomatoes

¼   ounce fresh basil, chopped

¾   cup warm water

1   teaspoon sea salt

2   tablespoons olive oil

      Dash black pepper

This colorful appetizer combines flavorful roasted red peppers with the zest of Greek feta cheese.

1. To prepare peppers, roast under a broiler until evenly charred. Place peppers in a paper bag or wrap in a damp towel for 15 minutes until cool enough to handle. Peel away charred skin and rinse well. Remove stems and seeds and cut peppers lengthwise into 8 strips 1¼ inches wide. Trim stem end of each strip to flatten top edge.

2. Cut feta cheese into thick matchsticks about 1½ to 2 inches long and ¼ inch thick.

3. Prepare appetizer by placing a pepper strip, outer side down, on a cutting board. Roll pepper around a sliver of cheese. Repeat with remaining peppers and feta.

4. To prepare dressing, soak sun-dried tomatoes in warm water for 20 minutes until soft. Combine tomatoes with remaining ingredients in a blender and puree until smooth. Drizzle over prepared peppers and serve.

Note: *To reduce calories, fat, and cholesterol, substitute low-fat mozzarella cheese for the feta.*

Calories per serving:	148
Grams of fat:	9.8
Percentage fat calories:	61%
Cholesterol:	40 mg.

Quesadillas

Yields 1 dozen

Prep Time: 10 minutes
Cooking Time: 10 minutes

3   corn chapatis or corn tortillas, quartered

1   cup grated Monterey Jack or mozzarella cheese

½   red bell pepper, cut into julienne strips

½   green or yellow bell pepper, cut into julienne strips

    Salsa, for garnish

Everyone has a favorite way to make quesadillas, but this is the easiest and fastest. You can't make too many of these — everyone loves them!

1.   Preheat oven to 375°F. Place chapatis on a cookie sheet and sprinkle with cheese. Top with peppers and bake 10 minutes until cheese is bubbling. Serve with salsa.

Calories per serving:	40
Grams of fat:	2.3
Percentage fat calories:	50%
Cholesterol:	7.5 mg.

Steamed Umeboshi Rice Balls

Yields 1 dozen

Prep Time: 20 minutes
Cooking Time: 20 minutes

1	cup basmati rice
5	umeboshi plums, pitted
1	tablespoon tamari
½	cup chopped scallions
1	garlic clove, minced
8	shiitake mushrooms, sliced
8	water chestnuts, sliced
1½	teaspoons minced fresh ginger

Pungent umeboshi plums (believed to regulate the body's acid balance and soothe jumpy stomachs) combine with fragrant basmati rice for these Oriental-inspired nibbles. Fresh shiitake mushrooms taste great; when using dried ones, soak until tender and drain well. The soaking liquid, strained through cheesecloth and heated, makes a restorative tea.

1. Soak rice in water to cover for at least 10 minutes. Meanwhile, combine plums, tamari, scallions, garlic, shiitake, water chestnuts and ginger in a blender or food processor and blend until smooth.

2. Drain rice and place on paper towels. Form plum mixture into 1-inch balls and roll each in rice. Place in a steamer basket such as a bamboo wok steamer, cover and steam over moderately high heat 20 minutes until firm.

Note: *Once the balls have been rolled in rice, they can be packed in layers (separated by waxed paper) in a plastic container and frozen. Remove from freezer 3 hours before serving and steam as directed.*

Calories per serving:	69
Grams of fat:	.2
Percentage fat calories:	3%
Cholesterol:	0 mg.

Norimaki Stacks

Serves 12

Prep Time: 15 minutes

3   cups quick-cooking
    brown rice, cooked

1   tablespoon brown rice
    vinegar

1   teaspoon wasabi,
    dissolved in 1 tablespoon
    tamari

2   tablespoons sesame seeds

1   cup steamed vegetables
    such as carrots and bell
    peppers sliced lengthwise

3   whole nori sheets

    Additional tamari for
    dipping, if desired

Even the less-than-dexterous sushi lover can make this dish, which we call "sushi lasagna." The brown rice and vegetable filling — mixed with wasabi powder for a fiery horseradish kick — is layered with whole sheets of nori and then cut into serving pieces.

1. In a medium bowl, combine rice, vinegar, wasabi and sesame seeds.

2. Spread ⅓ of the rice mixture in an 8-inch square pan. Arrange ⅓ of the vegetables over rice layer and top with a sheet of nori. Continue layering remaining ingredients, ending with nori.

3. To serve, cut into wedges or squares. If desired, serve with additional tamari for dipping.

Calories per serving:	95
Grams of fat:	1.2
Percentage fat calories:	11%
Cholesterol:	0 mg.

Great Greens

Great Greens!

No matter how you toss it, there are plenty of reasons to put salads on the table all year long. Extend your salad repertoire into winter with seasonal produce, grains, pasta and legumes. Our tangy Dilled Winter Potato Salad (page 84) and Pear And Onion Salad With Chutney (page 75) are sumptuous combinations of fall fruits and vegetables that add pizazz to winter meals.

Here are some hints to keep in mind when preparing your next salad:

- Use several types of lettuce, greens and fresh herbs such as basil.

- Add colorful, edible flowers such as nasturtiums found in the produce department at your natural foods store.

- Add crunch to salads with a sprinkling of nuts, chopped raw fruit and vegetables, or lightly toasted sesame, canola or sunflower seeds. For added crispness, top salads with seasoned popped wheat, natural salad topping blends or popcorn.

- Create your own salad dressings with your favorite ingredients. Combine an acid like vinegar, lemon juice or tomato juice with smooth-tasting ingredients such as oil, tahini or miso for a base. Season to taste with spices, fresh herbs, garlic, honey, tamari, mustard or other natural condiments.

- To reduce fat and calories in salad dressings, spice up low-fat ingredients such as miso, nonfat yogurt, stock or vegetable juice. Or dilute bottled salad dressing with water and transfer to a spray bottle. Spritz dressing on salad instead of pouring.

- Make healthy croutons with whole-grain bread. Brush bread slices lightly with olive oil or melted soy margarine and sprinkle with a natural spice blend before cutting into cubes. For a unique flavor, try Cajun spice blend, minced jalapeño peppers mixed with garlic powder, or instant miso soup and fresh ginger. Bake at 375°F for 15 minutes or until lightly toasted.

- For a light yet satisfying main course, add whole grains and legumes such as bulgur, millet, lentils or brown rice to a selection of seasonal vegetables.

Dairy-Free Caesar Salad

Serves 10

Prep Time: 10 minutes

Salad:

1½ pounds fresh mixed greens

¼ cup parsley, minced

Dressing:

2 tablespoons mellow miso

2 teaspoons mustard

⅛ teaspoon red pepper flakes

2 tablespoons lemon juice

2 garlic cloves, minced

5 tablespoons water

¼ cup Parmesan-style soy cheese (optional)

This all-time favorite doesn't suffer a bit from the deletion of high-cholesterol egg yolks. Use organic greens and parsley for an even better flavor.

1. Clean and dry greens. Combine in a large salad bowl with parsley. Cover with a clean kitchen towel and chill until just before serving.

2. In a small mixing bowl, combine miso, mustard, pepper flakes, lemon juice, garlic and water. Whisk well to blend. Just before serving, drizzle greens with dressing and sprinkle with Parmesan-style soy cheese if desired.

Note: *This colorful salad is featured on the cover.*

Calories per serving:	18
Grams of fat:	.4
Percentage fat calories:	20%
Cholesterol:	0 mg.

Summer Greens With Orange Plum Dressing

Serves 4 to 6

Prep Time: 15 minutes

Salad:

4   cups mixed salad greens such as lettuce, spinach and watercress

1   medium red onion, thinly sliced

1   medium orange, peeled and sectioned

Dressing:

2   teaspoons umeboshi paste or minced umeboshi

1   tablespoon olive oil

1   tablespoon fresh lime juice

⅔   cup freshly squeezed orange juice

2   tablespoons sesame tahini

    Freshly ground black pepper to taste

1   tablespoon toasted sesame seeds

You may have noticed the jars of pickled Japanese plums called umeboshi in the macrobiotic section of your store and wondered what to do with them. According to macrobiotic dietary principles, a bit of umeboshi every day helps keep the blood alkaline and neutralize acidity. In this refreshing salad, the plums' tartness is a delicious match for the sweet tang of oranges.

For other summer treats, rub an umeboshi over corn on the cob or mash one in guacamole for a tangy difference.

1. Toss greens, onion and orange in a large salad bowl.

2. In a blender or food processor, combine umeboshi, oil, juices, tahini and pepper or whisk together until thickened.

3. Just before serving, pour dressing over salad and sprinkle with sesame seeds.

    Note: *To lower fat calories in this recipe to 29%, eliminate sesame seeds and reduce tahini to 1 tablespoon.*

Calories per serving:	152
Grams of fat:	7.6
Percentage fat calories:	45%
Cholesterol:	0 mg.

Winter Sunshine Salad

Serves 2

Prep Time: 10 minutes

Salad:

1   bunch watercress,
    stemmed

2   Belgian endives, leaves
    separated

2   thin slices red onion

1   orange, peeled and
    segmented

Dressing:

1   cup nonfat plain yogurt

    Zest and juice of
    1 orange

    Freshly ground black
    pepper to taste

This refreshing arrangement of fresh winter produce will enliven any meal.

1. Arrange watercress and large leaves of endive on two salad plates. Chop remaining endive and distribute evenly between the two plates.

2. Cut each slice of onion in half. Place onion slivers and orange segments on top of chopped endive. Drizzle dressing over all before serving.

3. To make dressing, combine yogurt, orange juice and zest, and black pepper.

Calories per serving:	*232*
Grams of fat:	*1.6*
Percentage fat calories:	*6%*
Cholesterol:	*0 mg.*

Wilted Red Cabbage & Apple Salad

Serves 6

Prep Time: 10 minutes
Cooking Time: 15 to 20 minutes

3   onions, chopped

¼   cup red wine vinegar

½   cup vegetable broth

2   pounds red cabbage, coarsely shredded

¼   teaspoon caraway seed

2   Granny Smith apples, peeled, cored and diced

¼   teaspoon freshly ground black pepper

Wilted salads are very chic, and this version is especially easy since it's cooked in vegetable broth. A healthful, vitamin A-rich combination of cabbage, apple and seasonings, this salad is a unique and tasty dish.

1. In a medium saucepan, cook onions over moderate heat with vinegar and vegetable broth until soft, about 10 minutes.

2. Stir in cabbage, caraway seed, apples and pepper, cover and cook 5 to 10 minutes until cabbage is slightly tender but still crisp.

Calories per serving:	*120*
Grams of fat:	*.6*
Percentage fat calories:	*5%*
Cholesterol:	*0 mg.*

Pear & Onion Salad With Chutney

Serves 2

Prep Time: 10 minutes

Salad:

2   ripe pears, cored and halved

1   small bunch watercress

8   thin slices red onion

Chutney:

1   10-ounce jar peach preserves

½   teaspoon grated fresh ginger

⅓   cup seedless raisins

¼   cup snipped dried apples

½   garlic clove, finely minced

1   tablespoon apple cider vinegar

1   tablespoon fresh lemon juice

1   teaspoon sea salt

¼   teaspoon cinnamon

½   teaspoon freshly ground black pepper

The sweetness of pears combined with peppery watercress and pungent onion makes an unusual and eye-appealing salad. Look for Bartlett, Comice or Bosc pears for a naturally sweet taste.

1. Arrange pears, watercress and onion on salad plates. Garnish with chutney.

2. To make chutney, combine peach preserves with remaining ingredients. Set aside chutney for at least an hour before serving to allow flavors to mingle.

Calories per serving:	418
Grams of fat:	1
Percentage fat calories:	2%
Cholesterol:	0 mg.

Cucumber Fruit Salad
With Chili-Mint Dressing

Serves 4 to 6

Prep Time: 10 minutes

Dressing:

¾ cup nonfat plain yogurt

¼ cup minced fresh mint

1 jalapeño or hot chili pepper, minced

½ teaspoon cumin

Salad:

Red leaf lettuce
for lining plate

2 cups diced pineapple

2 sliced peaches or papaya

2 cups seedless grapes

1 cucumber, sliced

⅓ cup minced scallion greens

Here's a cool salad combination of sweet and savory flavors that's smooth and spicy and very low in calories.

1. In a large bowl, combine yogurt, mint, pepper and cumin.

2. Line a serving plate or shallow bowl with lettuce. Arrange cucumber and fruit on top of lettuce and top with dressing. Sprinkle with minced scallions.

Calories per serving:	149
Grams of fat:	.8
Percentage fat calories:	5%
Cholesterol:	0 mg.

Fruit Salad Bowl-In-One

Serves 2

Prep Time: 10 minutes

1   cantaloupe, halved and scooped out, with the flesh cut into chunks

1   cup halved strawberries

1   cup seedless green grapes

½   cup granola

     Tropical-blend juice to moisten

The appearance of juicy cantaloupes in the produce department heralds the season for refreshing fruit salads. This one, made substantial with granola or other natural cereal, is a great snack on a warm day.

1. In a medium bowl, combine cantaloupe, strawberries, grapes and granola with just enough juice to moisten. Repack into cantaloupe halves and wrap in foil or plastic until ready to eat.

Calories per serving:	296
Grams of fat:	6
Percentage fat calories:	18%
Cholesterol:	0 mg.

Sunny Slaw

Serves 6

Prep Time: 15 minutes
Marinating Time: 4 hours

Dressing:

½   cup apple juice
     concentrate

1   teaspoon ground
     cinnamon

2   whole star anise

4   whole cloves

2   tablespoons lemon juice

Salad:

¼   cup dried apples,
     shredded

2   fresh apples, sliced

1   cup berries

1   cup melon balls

1   kiwi fruit, sliced

This sweet temptation makes a healthy summer treat. Take advantage of the season's bountiful offering of fresh organic fruit. Organic frozen apple juice concentrate adds just the right amount of sweetness to this spicy salad.

1. Combine juice concentrate, spices and lemon juice in a small saucepan. Bring to a boil and simmer until thickened, about 5 minutes. Remove from heat and cool completely.

2. Combine fruit in a serving bowl. Pour cooled juice mixture over fruit and toss. Refrigerate, tossing occasionally for at least 4 hours.

Calories per serving:	*116*
Grams of fat:	*.5*
Percentage fat calories:	*3.6%*
Cholesterol:	*0 mg.*

Gingered Carrot Salad On Rice Cakes

Serves 2

Prep Time: 10 minutes

2   **carrots, grated (about 2 cups)**

1   **cup nonfat plain yogurt**

½   **cup seedless raisins**

1   **teaspoon minced fresh ginger**

    Rice cakes

The praises of carrots hardly need singing. Carrots have 10 times more vitamin A than a peach and 30 times more than an egg. They provide calcium, potassium and fiber as well. They really shine in this spicy salad, which makes a great meal for dieters.

1. In a medium bowl, combine carrots, yogurt, raisins and ginger and mix well. Spread on rice cakes and enjoy.

Calories per serving:	145
Grams of fat:	.2
Percentage fat calories:	1%
Cholesterol:	0 mg.

Spicy Beet Salad

Serves 8

Prep Time: 30 minutes

Salad:

1	pound beets
⅓	pound snow peas
1	head radicchio
2	cups alfalfa sprouts
½	cup water chestnuts, sliced
3	scallions, minced

Dressing:

1	ounce pickled ginger
2	tablespoons tahini
1½	tablespoons mellow miso
½	teaspoon red pepper flakes
¼	teaspoon black pepper
¾	cup water
2	tablespoons cilantro, minced

This is a colorful salad with red beets and radicchio, green snow peas and white water chestnuts.

1. Peel and slice beets. Place in a steamer basket over rapidly boiling water, cover and cook until tender, about 8 minutes. Remove from steamer, strain and cool under cold running water.

2. Remove and discard stem end and string from snow peas. Steam, covered, over rapidly boiling water about 1 minute or until bright green. Remove from steamer, strain and cool under cold running water.

3. Arrange ring of radicchio leaves around edge of serving platter. Overlap radicchio with ring of sprouts, then fan beet slices over sprouts. Arrange water chestnuts over beets. Place snow peas in center of platter and sprinkle entire salad with minced scallions. Chill until ready to serve.

4. Pour liquid from ginger into a small mixing bowl. Mince ginger slices and add to bowl along with remaining dressing ingredients. Mix well. Serve dressing on the side.

Note: *To lower fat calories in this recipe to 25%, use only 1 tablespoon tahini.*

Calories per serving:	*61*
Grams of fat:	*2.4*
Percentage fat calories:	*35%*
Cholesterol:	*0 mg.*

Graceful Ginger Broccoli Salad

Serves 6

Prep Time: 15 minutes
Cooking Time: 7 minutes

Salad:

4   dried shiitake mushrooms

1   bunch broccoli

¼   pound fresh mushrooms, sliced

½   cup diced carrots

3   tablespoons toasted sesame seeds

Dressing:

¼   cup pickled ginger

3   tablespoons reserved pickled ginger juice

¼   cup tahini

2   teaspoons tamari

So simple to make, this is a very tasty combination. Steamed slices of broccoli and shiitake mushrooms are tossed with a pickled ginger dressing and topped with toasted sesame seeds.

1. Soak shiitake mushrooms in hot water 30 minutes. Drain and squeeze dry, then slice. Cut broccoli into florets and steam with shiitakes until tender. Refresh under cold water and transfer to a mixing bowl. Add fresh mushrooms, carrots, sesame seeds and toss.

2. Drain 3 tablespoons juice from ginger package into a small bowl. Mince ginger and add to bowl with tahini and tamari. Pour over vegetables and toss.

Note: *To cut fat calories in half, use only 1 tablespoon sesame seeds. Reduce tahini to 1 tablespoon and mix with 3 tablespoons water before adding to dressing.*

Calories per serving:	138
Grams of fat:	9
Percentage fat calories:	59%
Cholesterol:	0 mg.

Sesame Confetti Slaw

Serves 8 to 10

Prep Time: 15 minutes
Marinating Time: 1 hour

Dressing:

¼   cup vegetable oil

¼   cup toasted sesame oil

½   cup cider vinegar

¼   cup honey

1   tablespoon tamari

1   teaspoon wasabi powder
    or prepared mustard

Salad:

1   large (2½ pounds) green
    cabbage, shredded

1   small (½ pound) red
    cabbage, shredded

2   medium carrots, coarsely
    grated

1   medium red onion,
    shredded

1   green bell pepper, seeded
    and coarsely chopped

¼   cup toasted sesame seeds

This nourishing summer salad keeps very well in the refrigerator for at least a week. It adds a lively flavor to sandwiches, turkey hot dogs and grain burgers.

1. In a small saucepan, combine oils, vinegar and honey and bring to a boil over moderately high heat. Remove from heat and stir in tamari and wasabi.

2. In a large bowl, combine red and green cabbage, carrots, onion and pepper. Pour hot oil mixture over vegetables and mix well. Cover and refrigerate until chilled. If desired, drain off some of the marinade after chilling. Sprinkle with sesame seeds just before serving.

Note: *To cut fat calories in half, substitute 1 teaspoon miso dissolved in ½ cup warm water for vegetable oil, reduce sesame oil to 2 tablespoons and sesame seeds to 1 tablespoon.*

Calories per serving:	255
Grams of fat:	18
Percentage fat calories:	63%
Cholesterol:	0 mg.

Peppy Potato Salad

Serves 6

Prep Time: 15 minutes
Cooking Time: 8 minutes
Marinating Time: 20 minutes

1   pound red potatoes

1¾ cups diced jicama or
      apple

¾   cup salsa

1   teaspoon ground cumin

4   green onions, minced

¼   cup minced cilantro

How about a light and healthy alternative to a summertime favorite? Our oil-free potato salad is a perfect combination of potatoes and crunchy jicama, a sweet Mexican root vegetable, tossed with salsa and fresh cilantro.

1. Scrub potatoes and cut into 1-inch cubes. Place in a steamer basket over boiling water and steam until just cooked through, 10 to 12 minutes.

2. Drain potatoes and cool under running water. Combine with remaining ingredients and marinate 20 minutes.

Calories per serving:	82
Grams of fat:	.2
Percentage fat calories:	2%
Cholesterol:	0 mg.

Dilled Winter Potato Salad

Serves 6

Prep Time: 15 minutes
Cooking Time: 20 minutes

8	red potatoes, cut into 1½-inch chunks
2	tablespoons vegetable oil
2	celery stalks, thinly sliced
3	small radishes, sliced
2	medium carrots, grated
1	green bell pepper, cut into 1-inch strips
1	bunch scallions, sliced
⅓	cup fresh parsley, minced
¼	cup herb or apple cider vinegar
2	tablespoons Dijon-style mustard
½	package no-oil dressing mix
2	tablespoons chopped fresh dill
	Cherry tomatoes and grated cheddar cheese for garnish

Bet you never thought of using your wok to make potato salad! This warm, tangy dish, which contributes potassium and vitamin C to your diet, is perfect for fast meals.

1. In a large wok, bring 2 quarts water to a boil over high heat. Add potatoes, reduce heat to moderate and cook 15 minutes until potatoes are tender but still firm.

2. Drain potatoes and set aside. Return wok to moderately high heat. Add oil and heat until almost smoking.

3. Add celery, radish, carrots, pepper, scallions and parsley and stir-fry 2 minutes.

4. Add potatoes, mustard, vinegar and dressing mix and stir-fry 1 minute until heated through. Stir in dill.

5. To serve, garnish with cherry tomatoes and a sprinkling of grated cheddar cheese.

Calories per serving:	243
Grams of fat:	6.8
Percentage fat calories:	25%
Cholesterol:	5 mg.

Sweet & Spicy Quinoa

Serves 6

Prep Time: 20 minutes
Cooking Time: 20 minutes

1½ cups quinoa

½ teaspoon sea salt

¼ teaspoon turmeric

¼ teaspoon fennel seeds

¼ teaspoon ground cardamom

¼ teaspoon ground cumin

1 3-inch cinnamon stick

3 quarter-sized slices ginger

2 dried red chilies

3 cups water

¼ cup seedless raisins

Radicchio and alfalfa sprouts for garnish

This is an exotic main-dish salad that can be eaten hot or cold.

1. Rinse quinoa in several changes of cold water until water runs clear. Drain and transfer to a saucepan. Add salt, spices, chilies and water. Bring to a boil. Reduce heat, stir once, cover and simmer until water is absorbed and quinoa is just tender, 18 to 20 minutes.

2. Remove cooked quinoa from heat and stir in raisins. Set aside about 10 minutes for raisins to plump. Serve on a bed of radicchio surrounded with alfalfa sprouts.

Calories per serving:	*216*
Grams of fat:	*3.4*
Percentage fat calories:	*14%*
Cholesterol:	*0 mg.*

Rice Latino

Serves 6

Prep Time: 15 minutes
Cooking Time: 15 minutes

3   cups cooked brown rice

2   teaspoons olive oil

¾   cup salsa

½   cup pasta sauce

1½ cups chickpeas, drained if bottled

½   cup black olives

2   tablespoons chopped fresh basil or cilantro

You can use leftovers, natural brown and wild rice blends, or quick-cooking plain brown rice for this savory dish. Enjoy it warm with a garnish of bell pepper rings or cold as a salad, perhaps in pita bread with crisp lettuce.

1. In a large bowl, toss rice with olive oil. Stir in salsa and pasta sauce and toss to coat rice evenly.

2. Add chickpeas, olives and basil and toss briefly. If desired, heat briefly in a saucepan before serving.

Calories per serving:	*222*
Grams of fat:	*4.6*
Percentage fat calories:	*19%*
Cholesterol:	*0 mg.*

Succotash Rice Salad

Serves 6

Prep Time: 15 minutes
Cooking Time: 10 to 15 minutes

1 cup instant brown rice, uncooked

¾ cup vinaigrette salad dressing

Kernels from 3 ears of steamed corn, about 1½ cups

5 medium radishes, halved and sliced

1 cup steamed lima or green beans

2 tablespoons chopped cilantro

¾ cup feta or other goat cheese, crumbled

Instant brown rice is the healthful time-saver here. For a light yet filling main dish, this salad can be used to stuff halved zucchini or cucumbers. You can also stuff it into whole wheat pitas with sprouts or lettuce and take it with you for lunch.

This colorful salad may be prepared ahead and refrigerated, but remove it from the refrigerator 15 minutes before serving and toss well to redistribute the dressing.

1. Cook instant brown rice according to package directions, 10 to 15 minutes. Drain and cool, then place in a large bowl and toss with half the vinaigrette dressing.

2. Add corn, radishes, beans, cilantro and feta cheese and toss with remaining dressing.

Note: *To reduce calories, cholesterol and fat in this recipe, use only ½ cup feta cheese. Substitute 2 tablespoons olive oil combined with ⅓ cup rice wine vinegar for vinaigrette dressing. Toss salad to coat grains evenly with dressing.*

Calories per serving:	*321*
Grams of fat:	*21*
Percentage fat calories:	*59%*
Cholesterol:	*16.7 mg.*

Hoppin' John Salad

Serves 16

Prep Time: 10 minutes

8 cups cooked black-eyed peas

2 cups chopped bell pepper, preferably a combination of red, yellow and green

1 cup chopped scallion, white and green parts

⅔ cup vinaigrette salad dressing

1 teaspoon hot red pepper flakes, or to taste

Hoppin' John is an old Southern dish traditionally made on January 1, with black-eyed peas (said to bring luck for the new year) and rice, plus a lively kick of hot pepper sauce. We've turned Hoppin' John into a salad with red, yellow and green bell peppers and scallions adding juicy crunch and flavor.

1. For help with preparing dried black-eyed peas, consult our "Adaptable All-Purpose Beans" chart on page 126.

2. Combine ingredients and toss until thoroughly mixed.

Calories per serving:	*153*
Grams of fat:	*5.8*
Percentage fat calories:	*34%*
Cholesterol:	*0 mg.*

Falafel-Stuffed Tomatoes

Serves 5

Prep Time: 20 minutes
Cooking Time: 15 minutes

5   **large ripe tomatoes**

1½   **cups falafel mix**

2   **tablespoons chopped fresh parsley**

½   **cup grated mild cheese such as mozzarella or Monterey Jack**

1   **tablespoon olive oil**

The spicy Middle Eastern chickpea mixture called falafel is sold in an easy-to-prepare mix. It is usually formed into balls and fried, but this new twist on the recipe is easier to prepare and perfect for a hot summer meal.

1. Cut tops off tomatoes and scoop out insides. Turn upside down on paper towels to drain. Cut seeded pieces of tomato flesh into cubes and set aside.

2. In a medium bowl, prepare falafel mix according to package directions by adding water and stirring well. Stir in reserved tomato chunks, parsley and cheese.

3. Preheat oven to 350°F. Place tomatoes in a shallow pan and stuff each with falafel mixture. Drizzle with olive oil and bake 15 minutes until tops are lightly browned.

Calories per serving:	265
Grams of fat:	9
Percentage fat calories:	17%
Cholesterol:	9 mg.

Perfect Protein Tabouli Salad

Serves 4

Prep Time: 20 minutes

1   package tabouli mix

¼   cup chopped fresh
      parsley

3   scallions, chopped

½   cup reconstituted, sliced
      sun-dried tomatoes

      Juice of 1 large lemon

1   cup drained, cooked
      pinto beans

This is a satisfying and healthful lunch dish made by adding pinto beans to prepared packaged tabouli salad. The beans complement the bulgur wheat amino acids, so you get the benefit of complete protein as well as good taste. Sun-dried tomatoes contribute a delightful tanginess.

1. Prepare tabouli mix according to package directions. Add parsley, scallions, sun-dried tomatoes, lemon juice and mix well.

2. Stir in beans, cover and refrigerate several hours, if possible, to let flavors blend.

Variations: *Any leftover steamed vegetables such as broccoli, carrots or cauliflower may be added to this salad, as can cooked sea vegetables like arame or hijiki. Substitute Great Northern or other cooked beans for pinto beans.*

Calories per serving:	*427*
Grams of fat:	*18.4*
Percentage fat calories:	*39%*
Cholesterol:	*0 mg.*

Maple, Bean & Tortellini Salad

Serves 8

Prep Time: 15 minutes

Dressing:

¼ cup olive oil

1 tablespoon brown rice vinegar

1 tablespoon lemon juice

¼ cup maple syrup

2 tablespoons water

2 small garlic cloves, minced

Salad:

10 ounces green tortellini or whole wheat pasta, cooked and drained

3 bell peppers, preferably 1 red, green and yellow, seeded and cut into julienne strips

1 cup cooked, drained Great Northern beans

1 bunch scallions, chopped

2 tablespoons chopped fresh basil or parsley

Vinaigrette dressing made with maple syrup will do wonders for summer salads, from simple lettuces to pastas and grains. Here, we used frozen whole wheat tortellini stuffed with cholesterol-free tofu, but cheese tortellini or any hearty whole wheat pasta shape also works.

1. In a blender or food processor, combine oil, vinegar, lemon juice, 2 tablespoons water, maple syrup and garlic and process until well-combined.

2. In a large bowl, toss pasta with dressing. Add peppers, beans, scallions and herbs and toss well before serving.

Calories per serving:	236
Grams of fat:	8.8
Percentage fat calories:	34%
Cholesterol:	0 mg.

West Indian Millet & Pasta Salad

Serves 4 to 6

Prep Time: 20 minutes

Salad:

2 cups cooked spinach pasta

1 cup cooked millet

1 red bell pepper, finely chopped

2 scallions, thinly sliced

1 tablespoon chopped fresh parsley

Dressing:

¾ cup vinaigrette salad dressing

2 tablespoons peanut butter

1 teaspoon honey

   Cayenne pepper to taste

6 slices peeled and cored fresh pineapple

2 large navel oranges, peeled and sectioned

½ cup dry-roasted peanuts

Millet is a small yellow grain with a light but hearty flavor, and it works well in many different recipes, from soups to puddings. Here, it's partnered with spinach pasta, fresh orange segments and peanuts. Because it takes less than half an hour to cook, it's a convenient grain to have on hand for last-minute meals.

1. In a large bowl, toss together pasta, millet, pepper, scallions and parsley.

2. Whisk together vinaigrette dressing, peanut butter, honey and cayenne. Pour over pasta mixture. Garnish with pineapple, oranges and peanuts.

Note: *Reduce calories and fat in this recipe by cutting peanut butter in half and eliminating peanuts. Use only ½ cup vinaigrette salad dressing.*

Calories per serving:	472
Grams of fat:	25.8
Percentage fat calories:	49%
Cholesterol:	0 mg.

Soba & Adzuki Salad With Spicy Plum Dressing

Serves 3 to 4

Prep Time: 15 minutes

<u>Dressing:</u>

2   umeboshi plums, pitted

2   tablespoons lemon juice

1   tablespoon brown rice vinegar

1   tablespoon toasted sesame oil

1   teaspoon wasabi powder

     Dash of tamari

<u>Salad:</u>

1   package soba noodles, cooked and drained

1   cup cooked adzuki beans

3   scallions, green part only, sliced on the diagonal

2   tablespoons sesame seeds

Dark red adzuki beans are small, tasty and very easy to digest. They need to be soaked before cooking, so it pays to make a large batch, but take care not to overcook them. Leftovers can be refrigerated or frozen and can be mixed into casseroles, soups, pâtés, stuffings or croquettes.

1.   In a blender, combine plums, lemon juice, vinegar, sesame oil, wasabi, tamari and 2 tablespoons water and blend until creamy, about 1 minute.

2.   In a large bowl, combine noodles and adzuki beans.

3.   Toss dressing with noodles and adzuki beans. Garnish with scallions and sesame seeds.

Calories per serving:	380
Grams of fat:	8
Percentage fat calories:	19%
Cholesterol:	0 mg.

Spicy Noodle Salad With Hijiki

Serves 6

Prep Time: 20 minutes

Salad:

½   cup hijiki or arame

1   package soba noodles, cooked and drained

2   medium carrots, sliced

3   scallions, sliced

4   celery stalks, sliced

Dressing:

¼   cup tahini

½   cup brewed bancha or caffeine-free dark tea

3   tablespoons tamari

1   teaspoon cayenne pepper

1   tablespoon toasted sesame oil

1   tablespoon honey

1   tablespoon rice vinegar

3   garlic cloves, minced

This dramatic-looking and wonderfully spiced Asian noodle dish is made of Japanese soba (buckwheat) noodles in a nutty, Chinese-inspired sauce. The ingredient list looks long, but the dish is quickly assembled. Serve warm or cool. If you do refrigerate it, let it stand at room temperature for an hour before serving.

1. Briefly rinse hijiki, then soak in a bowl of water for 10 minutes until softened. Drain and place in a large bowl. Add noodles, carrots, scallions and celery and toss well to combine.

2. In a small bowl, stir together tahini, tea, tamari, cayenne pepper, sesame oil, honey, rice vinegar and garlic. Pour dressing over noodle mixture and toss to coat evenly.

Calories per serving:	262
Grams of fat:	8.4
Percentage fat calories:	29%
Cholesterol:	0 mg.

Shrimp & Sugar-Snap Salad

Serves 8 to 10

Prep Time: 20 minutes
Marinating Time: 1 hour

Salad:

2	dozen large shrimp, lightly cooked, shelled and deveined
½	pound sugar-snap peas
2	cucumbers, peeled, sliced
4	celery stalks, sliced
4	cups cooked whole wheat couscous (1⅓ cups raw)

Dressing:

2	tablespoons vegetable oil
⅓	cup cider or wine vinegar
⅓	cup water
1	tablespoon mustard
2	tablespoons toasted sesame oil
3	tablespoons tamari
1	tablespoon honey
	Sea salt and freshly ground pepper to taste

The delicate colors of this main-dish salad, tossed in a snappy mustard vinaigrette, look particularly lovely on a bed of pale yellow couscous.

1. In a large bowl, combine shrimp, peas, cucumber and celery. Whisk together dressing ingredients and pour over shrimp mixture. Cover and refrigerate 1 hour before serving.

2. To serve, place couscous on a large platter. Spoon shrimp salad on top.

Note: *Snow peas may be substituted for sugar-snap peas in this recipe.*

Calories per serving:	224
Grams of fat:	8.6
Percentage fat calories:	35%
Cholesterol:	34 mg.

Teriyaki Chicken Salad

Serves 6

Prep Time: 20 minutes
Cooking Time: 8 minutes
Marinating Time: 2 hours

2   boneless, skinless
    chicken breasts

½   cup tamari

⅓   cup mirin

2   tablespoons honey

1   cup nonfat plain yogurt

1   teaspoon spicy mustard

1   teaspoon garlic, minced

3   tablespoons cilantro,
    minced

1   cup instant brown rice

1½ cups chicken stock

½   teaspoon sea salt

½   cup red and green bell
    pepper, sliced

4   scallions, minced

2   cups lettuce, shredded

1   tablespoon toasted
    almonds, chopped

This hearty main-course salad uses mirin, a Japanese cooking wine made from rice, to create a sweet flavor that enhances the chicken.

1. Chill chicken stock and discard fat. Place chicken on cutting board and pound with a meat tenderizer or the flat side of chef's knife to an even ½-inch thickness. Put in a shallow baking dish. Combine tamari, mirin and honey. Reserve 2 tablespoons and pour remainder over chicken. Turn meat to coat, then marinate in refrigerator 2 hours.

2. Whisk yogurt, mustard, garlic and cilantro into reserved tamari mixture. Prepare rice with chicken stock and salt according to package directions. When cooked, combine rice with yogurt dressing. Stir in peppers and scallions and mix well. Chill covered until ready to serve.

3. Place chicken on broiling rack about 4 inches from element. Broil, turning once and basting with marinade several times until cooked through, about 10 minutes. Arrange lettuce on serving platter and top with rice mixture. Slice chicken and place on top of rice. Garnish with chopped almonds.

Calories per serving:	301
Grams of fat:	5.4
Percentage fat calories:	16%
Cholesterol:	57 mg.

Salad Days Chicken

Serves 4 to 6

Prep Time: 5 minutes
Cooking Time: 10 minutes
Marinating Time: 1 hour

2   boneless, skinless chicken breasts

½   cup vinaigrette or other salad dressing

2   tablespoons lime juice

1   garlic clove, minced

All it takes is ½ cup of any natural salad dressing to tenderize and "flavor-ize" low-fat, boneless chicken breast halves. You can grill, broil or sauté them in a nonstick pan and then chop for salads or chill for a satisfying sandwich filling.

1. Arrange chicken in a shallow, nonmetallic pan in a single layer. Combine remaining ingredients with 2 tablespoons water and pour over chicken. Cover with plastic wrap and refrigerate at least one hour or overnight.

2. Grill, broil or sauté chicken 5 minutes on each side, taking care not to overcook.

Calories per serving:	*130*
Grams of fat:	*4.3*
Percentage fat calories:	*29%*
Cholesterol:	*56 mg.*

Oat Bran Tuna Salad

Serves 6

Prep Time: 15 minutes

1	6½-ounce can tuna, drained
1	cup drained, cooked Great Northern beans
½	cup chopped scallions
½	cup sliced bok choy or Chinese cabbage
2	tablespoons nonfat plain yogurt
2	teaspoons mustard
4	teaspoons fresh lime juice
½	cup watercress sprigs
¼	cup unsweetened, ready-to-eat oat bran cereal
	Crumbled nori, for garnish

Unsweetened, ready-to-eat oat bran cereal adds excellent crunch and valuable fiber to this salad — in fact, try sprinkling it wherever you'd toss some croutons or crumbled corn chips. If you're making the salad ahead of time, add the oat bran at the last minute for maximum crispness.

1. In a medium bowl, combine tuna, beans, scallions and bok choy and toss well.

2. In a small bowl, whisk together yogurt, mustard and lime juice. Pour over tuna mixture and toss to combine. Before serving, toss with watercress and oat bran cereal. Garnish, if desired, with crumbled nori.

Calories per serving:	*87*
Grams of fat:	*1.2*
Percentage fat calories:	*12%*
Cholesterol:	*16 mg.*

Soup's On!

Soup's On

On a long, cold winter evening, nothing satisfies your hunger and warms your soul like a steaming bowl of savory vegetable soup. And when you're sweltering in the summer heat, nothing picks you up like an icy cup of fresh fruit soup.

Naturally low in fat and high in vitamins, minerals and fiber, soups fulfill a number of roles. While all of the recipes we've included can be accompaniments to any meal, each is hearty and satisfying enough to be a meal on its own. Cook up our creamy Cauliflower Soup With Salsa Swirl (page 102) the next time you're expecting company for lunch; serve it with crunchy Blue Bayou Corn Sticks (page 48) and sit back and enjoy the compliments.

If you need more convincing of the virtues of soups, consider this: They're easy to prepare. All you have to do is chop vegetables, toss them in a pot of water or broth along with seasonings, grains or beans and let them simmer to perfection. We've even simplified some of the old classics like French Onion Soup (page 104). Instead of waiting hours for the soup's flavor to develop, we sprinkled in a package of natural vinaigrette dressing mix to give it instant character.

Of course, a soup like our Multi Bean Soup (page 111), which features no less than nine varieties of peas, beans, and grains, requires a bit of preplanning. But you can throw the assorted beans in a pot of water the evening before, soak them overnight and have them ready to cook the next morning.

As you browse our soup recipes, you'll discover other wonderful shortcuts, along with fat-trimming cooking techniques and suggestions for savory substitutes. For instance, we've found that if you refrigerate cans of chicken broth before pouring them into the soup pot, the chicken fat will solidify and rise to the surface, making it easy for you to skim it off. And if you prefer not to use chicken broth, use miso, tamari, or sea vegetables like wakame or kombu to flavor your soups.

Curried Amber Squash Bisque

Serves 4

Prep Time: 10 minutes
Cooking Time: 10 minutes

3 cups cooked, peeled squash (1½ pounds uncooked butternut or acorn squash)

1½ cups apple juice

½ cup applesauce

1 tablespoon curry powder

½ teaspoon minced garlic

Apples and squash make luscious partners in the soup tureen, as you'll taste in the first spoonful of this golden puree. Natural apple juice and applesauce streamline the recipe considerably, and a curry spice blend adds an exotic depth of flavor.

1. Combine all ingredients in batches in a blender or food processor and puree until smooth. Pour into a saucepan and heat.

2. Serve with Fennel Biscuit Twists made by adding 1 tablespoon fennel seeds to a batch of your favorite biscuit dough. Instead of making round biscuits, cut dough into 4- x 2-inch strips and gently twist or braid into breadstick shapes. Brush lightly with beaten egg white and bake as directed.

Note: *Squash can be cooked speedily in a microwave oven — whole, sliced or diced. To cook whole, place on a paper plate, pierce skin in several spots and microwave on high until done to desired softness. Leftover cooked squash pulp can be pureed and frozen.*

Calories per serving:	*119*
Grams of fat:	*.4*
Percentage fat calories:	*3%*
Cholesterol:	*0 mg.*

Cauliflower Soup With Salsa Swirl

Serves 6

Prep Time: 10 minutes
Cooking Time: 15 minutes

4   cups instant vegetable
     broth or water

1   garlic clove, minced

1   medium onion, chopped

2   medium carrots, chopped

1   head cauliflower,
     separated into florets

1   cup nonfat dairy milk or
     1% fat soy milk

     Sea salt and freshly
     ground black pepper
     to taste

½   cup salsa, drained

Creamy soups needn't be made with cream to be rich, thick and satisfying. This nourishing cauliflower puree gets its velvety texture from soy milk, though you could substitute skim milk. The bright swirl of salsa puree pleases both the palate and the eye.

1. In a large saucepan, combine broth, garlic, onion, carrots and cauliflower over moderate heat. Cook 15 minutes until cauliflower is tender but still firm.

2. With a slotted spoon, remove most of the cauliflower mixture to a blender or food processor, in two batches if necessary. Add milk and puree until smooth, then return to the saucepan. Season with salt and pepper to taste.

3. Rinse the blender container and puree salsa until smooth. To serve, ladle soup into bowls and top with a swirl of salsa puree.

Calories per serving:	94
Grams of fat:	.7
Percentage fat calories:	7%
Cholesterol:	0 mg.

Split-Second Vegetable Soup

Serves 2

Prep Time: 5 minutes
Cooking Time: 7 to 10 minutes

1   tablespoon olive oil

1   garlic clove, minced

1   cup chopped raw vegetables

1   19-ounce can chicken broth

½   cup cooked pinto beans

½   cup cooked millet, brown rice, barley or whole wheat couscous

½   teaspoon basil, oregano, marjoram or Italian herb blend

    Sea salt and freshly ground black pepper to taste

We suggest using a mixture of zucchini, green beans and carrots in this soup, but almost any variation will do — providing a great use for leftover vegetables, grains or beans lurking in the refrigerator. Add a jar of naturally prepared beans from your pantry and sauté the garlic and vegetables in olive oil for a hearty homemade flavor.

1. In a medium saucepan, warm olive oil over moderate heat. Add garlic and vegetables and sauté 5 minutes, stirring occasionally.

2. Add chicken broth, beans, grains and seasonings. Reduce heat to moderately low and simmer 10 minutes until vegetables are tender but still firm.

Note: *To reduce fat in this recipe, first refrigerate the chicken broth, then skim off the congealed fat that rises to the top. Or substitute vegetable or miso broth for the chicken broth.*

Calories per serving:	*300*
Grams of fat:	*14.4*
Percentage fat calories:	*43%*
Cholesterol:	*5.4 mg.*

Spiced French Onion Soup

Serves 2

Prep Time: 15 minutes
Cooking Time: 20 minutes

1   large onion, thinly sliced

1   tablespoon vegetable oil

1   tablespoon whole wheat pastry flour

2   cups chicken or vegetable broth

1   envelope vinaigrette dressing mix

2   slices whole wheat bread

1   cup grated Monterey Jack cheese

What a delight to dig beneath the bubbling cheese topping into this spicy, warming soup. Packaged salad dressing is the shortcut to a rich flavor that usually takes hours of simmering to achieve.

1. In a medium saucepan, sauté onion in oil over moderate heat 5 minutes until softened. Add flour and stir until browned, about 5 minutes.

2. Preheat broiler. Add broth and dressing mix and stir to dissolve. Bring to a boil, then remove from heat.

3. Ladle soup into 2 ovenproof bowls and top each with a slice of bread. Sprinkle with cheese and broil till melted.

Note: *To lower fat content of this recipe, either eliminate cheese topping or use skim milk mozzarella instead of Monterey Jack cheese.*

Calories per serving:	*409*
Grams of fat:	*25.4*
Percentage fat calories:	*56%*
Cholesterol:	*42 mg.*

Mama's Escarole Soup

Serves 6

Prep Time: 20 minutes
Cooking Time: 30 minutes

1   tablespoon vegetable oil

1   medium onion, chopped

2   garlic cloves, minced

2   celery stalks, chopped

3   large tomatoes, chopped

2   large potatoes, diced

7   cups vegetable broth, or use instant vegetable bouillon cubes

1   tablespoon chopped fresh parsley

1   teaspoon Italian herb blend, or ½ teaspoon each basil and oregano

    Sea salt and freshly ground black pepper to taste

1   pound escarole, washed, stemmed and chopped

    Grated Parmesan cheese for garnish

This light yet substantial vegetable soup is a time-honored Italian cure for spring head colds or whatever else ails you. Even if you're feeling fine, it makes a wonderful, simple lunch or supper dish.

1. In a large, nonstick saucepan, sauté onion and garlic in oil over moderate heat 5 minutes.

2. Add celery, tomatoes, potatoes, vegetable broth, parsley and seasonings and bring to a boil. Reduce heat to low and simmer, covered, 20 minutes.

3. Add escarole and simmer 10 minutes longer. Garnish with Parmesan cheese before serving.

Calories per serving:	117
Grams of fat:	2.7
Percentage fat calories:	21%
Cholesterol:	0 mg.

Stir-Fry Minestrone

Serves 6

Prep Time: 15 minutes
Cooking Time: 45 minutes

2	teaspoons vegetable oil
2	medium carrots, sliced
2	cups broccoli florets and stems, peeled and sliced
3	small zucchini, halved lengthwise and sliced
2	cups chopped fresh or frozen spinach
2	32-ounce jars pasta sauce
2	cups vegetable juice
3	cups water
½	pound whole-grain pasta shells, uncooked
2-4	garlic cloves, finely minced
1	tablespoon Italian herb blend
½	cup grated Parmesan
½	cup chopped fresh parsley

This nutritious and flavorful main-dish soup is as easy to prepare as a simple stir-fried vegetable dish. The crunchy vegetables provide vitamins A and C as well as fiber.

1. In a large wok, heat oil over high heat until almost smoking. Add carrot slices and stir-fry 2 minutes. Add broccoli and zucchini and stir-fry 2 minutes. Add spinach and stir-fry 1 minute.

2. Add pasta sauce, vegetable juice and 3 cups water, mixing until well combined. Stir in pasta shells. Bring soup to a boil, reduce heat to low and simmer, uncovered, 10 minutes.

3. Add garlic and Italian herb blend and simmer, covered, 10 minutes longer. Add parsley and simmer 3 minutes. To serve, sprinkle with Parmesan cheese.

Variations: *Use leftover pasta in the soup, adding it during the last 10 minutes of cooking time. To make an authentic Italian minestrone, add 1 cup cooked garbanzo or other beans in Step 3.*

Calories per serving:	335
Grams of fat:	6
Percentage fat calories:	16%
Cholesterol:	5.3 mg.

Warm Ways Hummus Soup

Serves 6

Prep Time: 10 minutes
Cooking Time: 20 minutes

1   tablespoon olive oil

2   medium onions, chopped

1   garlic clove, minced

1½ cups chicken or vegetable broth

3   cups, or one 24-ounce jar, cooked, drained chickpeas

1   teaspoon chopped fresh cilantro

    Juice of ½ lemon or 2 tablespoons lemonade

½   teaspoon black pepper

No matter how frantic your pace, slow down to sip this savory, soothing puree with flavors reminiscent of hummus, that delectable Middle Eastern chickpea spread. Whole-grain chips and sliced black olives make terrific soup garnishes.

1. In a heavy saucepan, warm oil over moderate heat. Add onions and garlic and sauté until onion is transparent, about 5 minutes.

2. Add chickpeas and broth and simmer 15 minutes. Let cool slightly, then puree in a blender or food processor until smooth. Return to saucepan and add cilantro, lemon juice and pepper.

Calories per serving:	208
Grams of fat:	6
Percentage fat calories:	25%
Cholesterol:	1 mg.

Creamy Curried Mung Bean Soup

Serves 6

Prep Time: 10 minutes
Cooking Time: 40 minutes

1	cup dried mung beans
7	cups water
3	dried red chilies
3	cloves garlic
1	3-inch cinnamon stick
½	teaspoon turmeric
¼	teaspoon ground coriander
¼	teaspoon ground cumin
¾	cup nonfat plain yogurt
2	cups diced mixed vegetables
¼	cup cilantro, minced

Serve this thick soup as a warming main course. Garnish with toasted chapatis or papadams and serve with a spicy chutney.

1. Combine beans, 6 cups water, chilies, garlic and spices in a pressure cooker. Bring to a boil and skim foam that rises to surface. Remove from heat and secure cooker top in place. Return to heat and bring to high pressure. Cook at this temperature 18 minutes.

2. Place cooker in sink and run cold water over top to release all pressure. Remove lid. Beat 1 cup water into yogurt and stir into soup. Return to stove and simmer 20 minutes, stirring frequently. Add vegetables (you can use fresh or leftover cooked vegetables) and cook to warm through. Stir in cilantro and serve.

Note: *To prepare this soup without a pressure cooker, simmer mung beans 35 minutes in Step 1.*

Calories per serving:	157
Grams of fat:	.5
Percentage fat calories:	3%
Cholesterol:	0 mg.

Festive Fava Soup

Serves 8

Prep Time: 10 minutes
Cooking Time: 35 minutes

1   cup leek or onion, chopped

5   cloves garlic, chopped

2   stalks celery, diced

1   tablespoon olive oil

6   tablespoons parsley, minced

2   16-ounce cans plum tomatoes, peeled

2   cups cooked fava or cannellini beans

8   cups water or vegetable stock

6   ounces elbow macaroni

1   teaspoon Italian herb blend

1   teaspoon sea salt

½   teaspoon black pepper

1   cup arugula (European salad green), chopped

¼   cup grated Parmesan

This savory soup features fava beans and pasta in a tomato broth. It's a quick and healthy weeknight dinner served with salad and bread.

1. Sauté leek, garlic and celery in olive oil 2 minutes. Stir tomatoes and half of the parsley into vegetables and simmer 10 minutes, stirring frequently. Add beans and continue to cook 5 minutes.

2. Add water and season with Italian herb blend, salt and pepper. Bring to a boil and simmer 10 minutes. Return to a boil and add pasta. Continue to cook soup until pasta is *al dente*.

3. Stir arugula into soup and warm briefly. Taste and adjust seasonings, adding more salt and pepper if necessary.

4. Transfer soup to a large serving bowl. Garnish with remaining parsley and Parmesan cheese.

Calories per serving:	*184*
Grams of fat:	*3*
Percentage fat calories:	*15%*
Cholesterol:	*2 mg.*

Multi Bean Soup Mix

Yields ten 2-cup packages

Prep Time: 15 minutes

1	pound barley
1	pound dried black beans
1	pound dried red beans
1	pound dried navy beans
1	pound dried Great Northern beans
1	pound dried lentils
1	pound dried split peas
1	pound dried black-eyed peas
1	pound dried pinto beans

Mix up this assortment of nutritious, natural beans ahead of time to shorten the soup's preparation time. Tuck a package of this savory bean soup mix, along with the following recipe, into your holiday food gifts. When the recipients taste its hearty flavor, you'll be sure to have their thanks.

1. Combine all beans in a large Dutch oven or roasting pan and mix well. Pick over to remove any stones. Divide into ten 2-cup portions and package in plastic bags or colorful fabric sacks and tie with ribbon or decorative twine. Glass canning jars may also be used.

Multi Bean Soup

Serves 6

Prep Time: 10 minutes
Soaking Time: 8 hours
Cooking Time: 90 minutes

2   cups **Multi Bean Soup Mix**

1   quart vegetable or chicken broth

1   medium onion, chopped

1   garlic clove, minced

    Sea salt and black pepper to taste

1   16-ounce can tomatoes, chopped, and juice

1   10-ounce can tomatoes and green chilies, undrained

1. The night before making soup, rinse beans and place in a Dutch oven. Cover with water and soak 8 hours.

2. Drain beans and add broth, onion, garlic, salt, pepper and a quart of water. Cover and bring to a boil, then reduce heat to moderately low and simmer 90 minutes until beans are tender. Just before serving, add tomatoes and chilies and heat through.

Calories per serving:	192
Grams of fat:	.6
Percentage fat calories:	3%
Cholesterol:	0 mg.

Fennel-Scented Chickpea Stew

Serves 6

Prep Time: 20 minutes
Cooking Time: 45 minutes

2	cups dried chickpeas
3	cloves garlic
2	tablespoons fennel seeds
¼	teaspoon nutmeg
½	teaspoon black pepper
2	dried chili peppers
1	teaspoon Italian herb blend
7	cups water
1	red bell pepper, sliced
1	zucchini, sliced
1	red onion, diced
1	fennel bulb, sliced
1	teaspoon sea salt, or to taste
¼	pound mushrooms, sliced
½	cup parsley, minced

This Mediterranean stew makes a delightful meal when served with a vegetable salad and bread. Or serve it over pasta or whole wheat couscous topped with grated Parmesan cheese.

1. Pick over beans and rinse well in several changes of water. Combine in pressure cooker with garlic, spices and water. Bring to a boil and skim foam that rises to surface. Remove from heat and secure cooker top in place. Return to heat and bring to high pressure. Cook at this temperature 30 minutes.

2. Place cooker in sink and run cold water over top to release all pressure. Remove lid. Stir in zucchini, red pepper, onion, fennel and salt and simmer uncovered 10 minutes, stirring occasionally. Add mushrooms and parsley and continue to cook 5 minutes. Taste and adjust seasonings.

Note: *To prepare this soup without a pressure cooker, first soak chickpeas overnight. Pour off soaking water and combine beans with garlic, spices and water in a pot. Cook approximately 1 hour until beans are tender but not mushy. Proceed with Step 2.*

Calories per serving:	243
Grams of fat:	3.4
Percentage fat calories:	13%
Cholesterol:	0 mg.

Early Spring Soup

Serves 4

Prep Time: 10 minutes
Cooking Time: 45 minutes

2   teaspoons toasted sesame
    oil

4   shiitake mushrooms,
    soaked in 1 cup water
    and sliced, with water
    reserved

1   medium onion, thinly
    sliced

1   6-inch piece of kombu

3   tablespoons tamari

2   tablespoons lemon juice

1   cup watercress

This is a classic kombu-based soup that's popular in Japan. To reconstitute shiitake mushrooms, soak for about an hour in warm water, then trim off the hard stems. Strain the soaking liquid through a double layer of dampened cheesecloth and add to the soup. It's also great as a revitalizing hot beverage.

1. In a medium saucepan, heat sesame oil over moderate heat. Add sliced shiitake mushrooms and onion and sauté 5 minutes.

2. Add shiitake mushroom soaking water, 5 cups cold water, kombu, tamari and lemon juice. Bring to a boil, reduce heat to moderately low and simmer 30 minutes.

3. Remove kombu and slice half of it thinly. (Reserve remaining kombu for another recipe.) Return sliced kombu to soup and cook 10 minutes. Remove from heat and stir in watercress.

Calories per serving:	82
Grams of fat:	2.4
Percentage fat calories:	26%
Cholesterol:	0 mg.

Hot, Sour & Delicious! Soup

Serves 4 to 6

Prep Time: 15 minutes
Cooking Time: 15 minutes

4   cups chicken broth or miso soup

1   teaspoon kuzu

2   garlic cloves, minced

½   teaspoon honey

½   teaspoon each sea salt and freshly ground black pepper

2   tablespoons Worcestershire sauce

2   tablespoons umeboshi or brown rice vinegar

1   tablespoon tamari

1   teaspoon toasted sesame oil

½   cup sliced shiitake mushrooms, presoaked if dried

½   cup cubed firm tofu

3   scallions, diced

Few dishes make you feel alive like a bowl of full-bodied hot and sour soup, one of the most popular Chinese take-out items. While the following ingredient list may look long, this delectable soup is easily and quickly assembled — it's just a matter of combining different flavors to create the unique character of this soup.

1. In a large saucepan, combine broth, kuzu, garlic, honey, salt and pepper, Worcestershire sauce, vinegar, tamari and sesame oil. Bring to a boil, then reduce heat to moderately low and add shiitake mushrooms.

2. Simmer gently 10 minutes, then add tofu and simmer 5 minutes longer. Garnish with scallions just before serving.

Note: *To reduce fat in this recipe, first refrigerate the chicken broth, then skim off the congealed fat that rises to the top. If you use miso broth as a base, the recipe will be practically fat free.*

Calories per serving:	157
Grams of fat:	10
Percentage fat calories:	58%
Cholesterol:	5 mg.

Celestial Miso Soup

Serves 2

Prep Time: 5 minutes
Cooking Time: 5 minutes

1   **6-ounce package instant miso soup**

       Hot pepper sesame oil, to taste

       Instant wakame

       Thin slivers of carrot, scallion, bell pepper and/or shiitake mushroom

Miso soup is a staple of many healthful eating styles, including the health-supporting macrobiotic diet. You can make it by stirring miso paste into hot (not boiling — it kills miso's beneficial digestive enzymes) water, or start with a powdered instant miso soup mix that may contain seasonings or sea vegetables such as wakame. Here we've enlivened the flavor with judicious dashes of hot pepper sesame oil.

1. Prepare instant miso soup according to package directions.

2. Bring soup to the simmer point (do not boil!) and add sesame oil, instant wakame and vegetables. Simmer until vegetables are crisp-tender, about 3 minutes.

Calories per serving:	*61*
Grams of fat:	*1.7*
Percentage fat calories:	*25%*
Cholesterol:	*0 mg.*

Summer Squash Soup With Curry

Serves 4

Prep Time: 15 minutes
Cooking Time: 20 minutes

1½ pounds yellow summer
    squash, chopped

1   large onion, chopped

1   teaspoon vegetable oil

2   tablespoons curry powder

1½ teaspoons grated ginger
    root

4   cups stock or water

⅓   cup 1% fat soy milk or
    nonfat plain yogurt

    Cilantro

This soup makes a lovely light supper served with grains or noodles and a salad.

1. In a large saucepan, sauté onion in oil. Add curry and stir. Add squash, water and ginger. Bring to a boil. Lower heat and simmer 20 minutes.

2. Puree soup in a blender with soy milk or yogurt (the yogurt adds more flavor). Gently reheat or chill and serve cold. Garnish with fresh cilantro before serving.

Calories per serving:	93
Grams of fat:	2
Percentage fat calories:	21%
Cholesterol:	0 mg.

Bombay Tomato Bisque

Serves 8

Prep Time: 10 minutes
Cooking Time: 20 minutes

6 cups spicy tomato juice

½ cup diced onion

2 carrots, diced

½ teaspoon ground cinnamon

¼ teaspoon ground coriander

½ teaspoon fennel seeds

Cayenne pepper to taste

1 cup diced cucumber

1½ cups water

½ cup fresh mint, minced

Nonfat plain yogurt

This delicate cold soup is guaranteed to cool your palate with the refreshing taste of fennel.

1. Combine tomato juice, onion, carrots and spices in a saucepan and bring to a boil. Cover and simmer until onion and carrot are tender, about 20 minutes.

2. Puree mixture in a food processor or blender. Stir in cucumber and water and chill completely. Serve garnished with mint and a dollop of yogurt.

Calories per serving:	45
Grams of fat:	.1
Percentage fat calories:	1%
Cholesterol:	0 mg.

Guacamole Soup

Serves 2 to 4

Prep Time: 10 minutes

1   ripe avocado, pureed

2   cups spicy tomato juice

¼   cup chopped cucumber

¼   cup chopped tomato

1   tablespoon chopped fresh cilantro

Summer produce like tomatoes and cucumber star in this cool, fast soup. Spicy tomato juice adds a kick and saves you the step of adding spices.

1. Stir together all ingredients or, if a smooth texture is desired, puree in a blender or food processor. Garnish with cilantro and additional chopped fresh vegetables.

Note: *To reduce the fat content of this recipe, substitute chopped carrots, red and green peppers, and celery for the avocado. Use slivers of avocado for garnish.*

Calories per serving:	200
Grams of fat:	15
Percentage fat calories:	68%
Cholesterol:	0 mg.

Berry Banana Bisque

Serves 6

Prep Time: 10 minutes

1   medium banana, peeled and sliced

1   cup sliced fresh strawberries

1½ cups nonfat plain yogurt

1   cup apple juice

1   cup berry juice such as strawberry or raspberry, or hibiscus cooler

This hyacinth-colored soup, based on nonfat yogurt, a banana and a few fresh strawberries, derives subtle flavor from natural organic apple juice.

1. In a blender or food processor, puree banana and strawberries. Pour into a bowl.

2. Stir in yogurt and juices until well-mixed. Refrigerate until ready to serve.

Calories per serving:	*100*
Grams of fat:	*.2*
Percentage fat calories:	*2%*
Cholesterol:	*0 mg.*

Minted Melon Berry Soup

Serves 4

Prep Time: 10 minutes

2   ripe cantaloupes, peeled
    and seeded

1   tablespoon chopped fresh
    mint

1   cup lime juice drink or
    limeade

    Dash of ground ginger

1   cup fresh blueberries

This makes a terrific breakfast on a hot summer morning. It's the best solution we know for using a couple of ripe melons.

1. Cut cantaloupes into chunks and puree in batches in a blender or food processor. Transfer to a serving bowl. Stir in lime juice, mint and ginger and gently add blueberries. Chill and serve cold.

Calories per serving:	_138_
Grams of fat:	_.9_
Percentage fat calories:	_6%_
Cholesterol:	_0 mg._

The Main Event

The Main Event: Wholesome Entrees

There are so many healthy, creative ways to serve a main dish. Whether your goal is speed and convenience or low-fat and cholesterol-free meals, you'll find great selections here. Our Fiery Tofu Fajitas (page 157) and our colorful Tomato-Couscous Ring With Vegetables (page 162) are quick-fix, low-fat favorites that our readers ask for again and again. These *Delicious!* entrees are guaranteed to please the pickiest eaters, and you can be assured that you're providing nutritious meals.

Wholesome products from your natural foods store such as beans, grains, soyfoods and organic produce are the staples of these recipes. For help with preparing grains, beans and soyfoods, consult our charts for cooking times and creative culinary ideas.

Some of our recipes call for chicken; when shopping, look for hormone-free, range-fed chickens. By supporting this industry, as well as organic growers and other natural foods producers, we are not only improving our own health, but also the health of the planet.

Soy! Oh Soy!

So many nutritious foods are made from soybeans. What are they and how do you use them? Here are some tips:

PRODUCT	DESCRIPTION	USES	STORAGE
TOFU	Curds from ground cooked soybeans drained and pressed into cubes. Firm and soft indicate density; silken indicates very smooth texture.	Firm: stir-fries, soups, salads; substitute for ground meat. Soft: dips, sauces, smoothies, pies, fillings; substitute for cottage or ricotta cheese.	Refrigerate in water up to 4 days after opening. Aseptically packaged tofu may be stored at room temperature before opening.
TEMPEH	Cracked whole bean that's cooked, fermented, incubated and steamed. Available in a variety of flavors.	Less crumbly than tofu and an excellent meat alternative. Good in stir-fries, stews, chili or spaghetti sauce.	Refrigerate up to 10 days or freeze up to 2 months.
TEXTURED VEGETABLE PROTEIN	Often referred to as TVP®, it's usually found in the bulk food section. Quality is very much like ground meat.	Use as a protein source in sauces, stews and casseroles. For each cup TVP® used, allow 1½ cups extra liquid.	Store in an airtight container up to 2 months.
MISO	Salted and fermented paste made from soy or other beans, or grains. Lighter colored misos tend to be lighter in flavor.	Use in soups and as a color or flavor enhancer in sauces, dips and spreads. Do not boil, or digestive enzyme is destroyed.	Best refrigerated. Keeps indefinitely.
SOY MILK	Noncurdled liquid from cooked, ground soybeans.	Use as a replacement for dairy milk. Substitute equal amounts for dairy milk in cooking and baking.	Refrigerate. Aseptically sealed cartons may be stored at room temperature before opening.
SOY CHEESE	Made like tofu, but more liquid is removed and a solidifier added. Available in many flavors including cheddar.	Use as you would any other cheese. Excellent in baked dishes.	Refrigerate.
TAMARI	Similar to soy sauce but thicker and more pungent. Traditionally wheat-free and made from miso brine.	Use for marinades, sauces and as you would soy sauce.	Store at room temperature for up to 6 months.

Bulk Grain Basics

This chart lists water proportions and cooking times for 1 cup of rinsed grain cooked in a covered pot or pressure cooker. When cooking 3 or more cups of grain, decrease water slightly. For porridge, use up to 5 cups water for each cup grain. If desired, ½-1 teaspoon sea salt may be added during cooking, except where noted.

GRAIN	CHARACTERISTICS	COOKING INSTRUCTIONS
AMARANTH	Tiny, beadlike seed that was an important food source in the ancient Aztec culture. Golden color and mild, nutty flavor. Becomes translucent as it cooks. High in protein, calcium, phosphorus and fiber, as well as lysine and methionine.	Add 1 cup amaranth to $1\frac{1}{2}$-$2\frac{1}{2}$ cups boiling water; cook 20 minutes. If pressure cooking, use $1\frac{1}{2}$ cups water and cook 10 minutes. Add salt after cooking. Yields 2 cups.
BARLEY	Available pearled, hulled and hulless. Color ranges from white to brown, depending on degree of milling. Chewy texture and earthy flavor. Although not as high in fiber as other grains, it's easier to digest.	Hulled or hulless: Add 1 cup barley to 3 cups boiling water; cook 60-90 minutes. If pressure cooking, use $2\frac{1}{2}$ cups water and cook 35-40 minutes. Pearled: Add 1 cup barley to $2\frac{2}{3}$ cups boiling water; cook 40 minutes. For pressure cooking, use 2 cups water; cook 25 minutes. Yields $3\frac{1}{2}$ cups.
BROWN RICE	A dependable source of B vitamins, vitamin E, iron, phosphorous, calcium, potassium, and fiber. Available in three basic forms: short grain (soft and sticky), medium (sweeter flavor, lighter texture) and long grain (drier, mild flavor). See our "Rice Roundup" chart (p. 128).	Add 1 cup rice to 2 cups boiling water; cover and cook 45 minutes. If pressure cooking, use $1\frac{1}{2}$ cups water and cook 20 minutes. Yields 3 cups.
BUCKWHEAT (KASHA)	Not a true grain, but the seeds of a plant related to belladonna. Most recipes that call for buckwheat mean kasha, its roasted form, which is available in whole groats and cracked grits. Reddish-brown color and robust, earthy flavor. Rich in vitamin E.	Add 1 cup buckwheat to 2 cups boiling water, cover and cook 10-12 minutes. Yields $3\frac{1}{2}$ cups.

GRAIN	CHARACTERISTICS	COOKING INSTRUCTIONS
MILLET	Small, yellow beadlike grain. Contains the most complete protein of all the grains; a good source of potassium, magnesium, phosphorous and B vitamins.	Add 1 cup millet to 2 cups boiling water; cook 30 minutes. If pressure cooking, use $1\frac{3}{4}$ cups water and cook 20 minutes. Yields 4 cups.
OATS	Available in a number of forms — Irish or steel-cut, rolled, flakes, quick-cooking and instant — which are familiar breakfast cereals. Lesser known whole oat groats make an excellent substitute for rice in soups and salads. Oat bran is reputed to be beneficial in lowering cholesterol in the bloodstream.	Whole oats: Stir 1 cup groats into 2 cups boiling water, cover and cook 1 hour. Rolled oats: Stir 1 cup oats into $2\frac{1}{4}$ cups boiling water; simmer uncovered 7-10 minutes. Irish oatmeal: Stir 1 cup steel-cut oats into 3 cups boiling water; simmer uncovered 30 minutes. Yields $2\frac{1}{2}$ cups.
QUINOA	Small, disk-shaped seed. Must be thoroughly rinsed before cooking to remove bitter resin coating. Contains 50% more protein than common grains, as well as higher levels of calcium, iron and B vitamins.	Add 1 cup quinoa to 2 cups boiling water; cover and simmer 15 minutes. For pressure cooking, use $1\frac{3}{4}$ cups water and cook 10 minutes. Yields $3\frac{1}{2}$ cups.
TEFF	Smallest whole grain on earth — it takes 17 grains to equal the weight of 1 grain of wheat. Reportedly contains 17 times more calcium than whole wheat. Best used in baked goods or as a hot cereal.	Stir 1 cup teff into 3 cups boiling water; simmer, uncovered, for 15 minutes, stirring occasionally to prevent lumps from forming. Yields 3 cups.
WHEAT	A reliable source of vitamin E, B vitamins, magnesium, phosphorus, protein and fiber. Available in several forms which make excellent substitutes for rice. Wheat berries are whole kernels with hulls removed. Cracked wheat is pulverized kernels with bran and germ intact. Bulgur is cracked wheat steamed and roasted. Couscous is tiny pastalike pellets made by processing the heart of the wheat kernel.	Wheat berries: Add 1 cup berries to 3 cups boiling water, cover and cook 2 hours. Add salt after cooking. If pressure cooking, use $2\frac{1}{2}$ cups water and cook 1 hour. Yields $2\frac{3}{4}$ cups. Cracked wheat: Stir 1 cup cracked wheat into 2 cups boiling water, cover and cook 20 minutes. Bulgur: Pour 2 cups boiling water over 1 cup bulgur, cover and let stand 20 minutes. Yields 3 cups. Couscous: Stir 1 cup couscous into $1\frac{3}{4}$ cup boiling water, remove from heat, cover and let stand 10 minutes. Yields $2\frac{3}{4}$ cups.

Adaptable, All-Purpose Beans

Dried beans must be soaked and rehydrated before cooking. Most varieties need to be soaked four hours; however, some thick-skinned beans such as soybeans need soaking overnight. Soak beans in plenty of water using three to four times as much water as beans. Change the soaking water occasionally to reduce the accumulation of gas. Drain beans after soaking and add fresh water before cooking. To reduce soaking time, boil beans for 2 minutes in 2 inches of water to cover then set aside. Beans will be ready for cooking in 1 hour. Pressure cooking also speeds the process because it allows you to skip presoaking. This chart gives pressure cooking times for soaked and unsoaked beans.

Hint: *To "de-gas" any kind of beans, add a bit of ginger or a strip of kombu (a broad-leaved sea vegetable) to the cooking pot.*

DRIED BEANS	CHARACTERISTICS	SOAKING & COOKING TIMES
ADZUKI (ADUKI)	Small, dark red bean native to the Orient. Easily digestible. Delicate, sweet flavor and light texture.	Soak 4 hours, cook 1 hour. Pressure cook soaked beans 5-9 minutes, unsoaked beans 14-20 minutes.
ANASAZI	Ancient Native American bean. Red-and-white speckled pinto-bean shape. Sweet, full flavor. Excellent in Mexican dishes.	Soak 4 hours, cook 1 hour. Pressure cook soaked beans 4-7 minutes, unsoaked beans 20-22 minutes.
BLACK (BLACK TURTLE)	A staple of Latin America and the Orient. Small, round purple-black bean. Excellent in soups, stews and bean cakes.	Soak 4 hours, cook 1½ hours. Pressure cook soaked beans 9-11 minutes, unsoaked beans 20-25 minutes.
BLACK-EYED PEA	Small, creamy-white bean with one black "eye." Traditional in Southern cooking. Good in soups and casseroles.	Soaking not required. Cook 45 minutes. Pressure cook 9-11 minutes.
CHICKPEA (GARBANZO)	Tan, round bean with a meaty, robust flavor. Traditional in the Middle East. Made into hummus and falafel. Good in soups and stews.	Soak 4 hours, cook 2 - 2½ hours. Pressure cook soaked beans 10-12 minutes, unsoaked beans 30-40 minutes.
FAVA (BROAD)	Pale to light brown, flat kidney-shaped bean. Tough skin should be removed after cooking. Popular in the Middle East and Italy.	Soak overnight, cook 3 hours. Pressure cook soaked beans 12-18 minutes, unsoaked beans 22-28 minutes.

DRIED BEANS	CHARACTERISTICS	SOAKING & COOKING TIMES
GREAT NORTHERN	Large, white, mild tasting bean with slightly granular texture. Used in Boston baked beans, casseroles and stews.	Soak 4 hours, cook 1 hour. Pressure cook soaked beans 8-12 minutes, unsoaked beans 25-30 minutes.
KIDNEY	Red bean named after its shape. Very tasty and versatile. Used in chili, salads, soups and stews.	Soak 4 hours, cook 1 hour. Pressure cook soaked beans 10-12 minutes, unsoaked beans 20-25 minutes.
LENTIL	Small, disk-shaped bean. Color varies. Excellent in soups, salads, Indian dals.	Soaking not required. Cook 30-40 minutes. Pressure cook 7-10 minutes.
LIMA	Flat bean that may be large or small. Buttery flavor and starchy texture. Ideal for casseroles.	Soak 4 hours, cook 1-1½ hours. Pressure cook soaked beans 4-7 minutes, unsoaked beans 12-16 minutes.
MUNG	Tiny, army-green bean sprouted for bean sprouts. Delightful rich flavor. Excellent in soups and dals.	Soaking not required. Cook 35-45 minutes. Pressure cook 10-18 minutes.
NAVY	Small, white all-purpose bean. Slightly granular texture. Ideal for baked beans and soups.	Soak 4 hours, cook 2 hours. Pressure cook soaked beans 9-12 minutes, unsoaked beans 22-25 minutes.
PEAS (SPLIT PEAS)	Available green or yellow (which is milder) and may be split or whole. Used in soups and dips.	Soaking not required. Cook 30 minutes. Pressure cook 20 minutes.
PINTO	Speckled light brown and rose-colored oblong bean commonly used in Southwestern and Mexican dishes.	Soak 4 hours, cook 1-1½ hours. Pressure cook soaked beans 8-12 minutes, unsoaked beans 25-30 minutes.
RED	Related to kidney and pinto beans. Mexican staple.	Soak 4 hours, cook 1-1½ hours. Pressure cook soaked beans 12-14 minutes, unsoaked beans 17-20 minutes.
SOYBEAN	One of world's most nutritious foods. Made into tofu, tempeh, miso. Very good in soups, stews.	Soak overnight, cook 3-3½ hours; pressure cook 45-50 minutes, presoaked soybeans only.

Rice Roundup

Rice is classified by variety and grain length. The outer husk is removed from all rice before it's marketed. Brown rice has only the husk removed and is more nutritious than white rice which has the bran, endosperm and germ removed.

To create the perfect pot of rice, follow these easy instructions: Rinse rice in several changes of cold water until water runs clear; transfer to a saucepan, add two parts liquid (water or stock) for one part rice, cover and bring to a boil; reduce to a simmer and cook until liquid is absorbed, about 35-40 minutes for most varieties.

BASMATI	Grown in India and other parts of the Far East. Alluring taste and aroma. Cooked grains remain separate and nonsticky.
TEXMATI™	Basmati rice grown in Texas. Similar to the traditional variety.
SHORT-GRAIN BROWN	Nutty, wholesome taste. Light and nonsticky, yet full-textured. Good for soups, side dishes and as an all-purpose rice.
SWEET BROWN	Deliciously sweet flavor and sticky texture. Excellent for puddings, casseroles and soups.
LONG-GRAIN BROWN	Nutty, wholesome taste and light texture. Good for salads, stir-fries and as an all-purpose rice.
MEDIUM-GRAIN BROWN	A cross between short- and long-grain brown rice.
KOKUKO ROSE	Mild, sweet flavor and sticky texture. Ideal for Oriental dishes, particularly sushi.
ARBORIO	Italian variety of sticky white rice. Perfect for risottos, puddings and casseroles.
RICE BLENDS	Prepackaged and bulk blends of rice such as wild and brown. Luscious blending of textures, tastes and aromas.
WILD RICE	Not a true rice, but a type of grass seed. Strong flavor and aroma. Can be treated like rice, though it must be cooked 15 to 20 minutes longer and requires additional liquid. Cook until seeds pop open. Good in stuffings, soups, salads and mixed with other rice varieties.

Preparing Perfect Pasta

Pasta is delicious, healthy and easy to prepare when you follow these helpful hints.

1. Bring a large pot of water to a rapid boil. To enhance flavor, toss in a sprig of your favorite fresh herb such as basil or oregano. Add 2 tablespoons olive oil to prevent pasta from sticking together while cooking. Or skip the oil and rinse cooked pasta under hot water instead.

2. Add pasta to boiling water and stir to separate. Fresh pasta is cooked 1-2 minutes after water returns to a boil. Dried pasta takes 7-15 minutes.

3. Cook pasta *al dente* or until just tender. Different shapes, drynesses and thicknesses take differing lengths of time to cook. Test pasta by removing a piece from water, cooling it under cold water and tasting to judge doneness.

Quick & Easy Pasta

Serves 4

Prep Time: 10 minutes
Cooking Time: 20 minutes

1	red onion, sliced
3	cloves garlic, sliced
2	teaspoons red pepper flakes
2	tablespoons olive oil
1	20-ounce can Italian plum tomatoes, drained
10	ounces whole-grain linguine
¼	cup fresh parsley, minced
	Sea salt and black pepper to taste

This recipe is a favorite of working people because it takes less than 30 minutes to prepare.

1. Sauté onions and garlic in olive oil over low heat until onion is wilted. Mix in pepper flakes and tomatoes. Simmer to thicken 10 minutes, stirring frequently.

2. Meanwhile, cook pasta *al dente* in 3 quarts rapidly boiling water. Drain and transfer to a large pasta bowl. Top with tomato sauce and parsley and toss to mix thoroughly. Serve immediately.

Calories per serving:	*357*
Grams of fat:	*8.5*
Percentage fat calories:	*21%*
Cholesterol:	*0 mg.*

Wok Spaghetti Tofu Toss

Serves 6

Prep Time: 20 minutes
Cooking Time: 25 minutes

1	pound whole-grain spaghetti or linguine
2	teaspoons vegetable oil
2	cups broccoli florets
2	red bell peppers, cut into thin 1-inch strips
1	package firm tofu, well-drained and cut into 1-inch cubes
3	large fresh mushrooms, thinly sliced
1	cup fresh basil, chopped
½	cup fresh parsley, chopped
1	can sliced black olives, well-drained
2-4	garlic cloves, minced
1	cup Italian salad dressing
½	teaspoon freshly ground black pepper
2	teaspoons Italian herb blend
⅓	cup grated Parmesan

This streamlined dish can be varied endlessly by substituting any number of vegetables or seasonings. Just be sure to simulate the beautiful contrast of colors presented here.

1. In a large wok, bring 3 quarts water to a boil over high heat. Add 1 teaspoon oil and spaghetti and cook 15 minutes until tender but still firm. Drain well and set aside.

2. Using a paper towel, rub the wok with 1 teaspoon oil and heat until smoking. Add broccoli and stir-fry 2 to 3 minutes. Add red pepper and stir-fry 1 minute longer.

3. Add tofu, mushrooms, basil, parsley, olives and garlic and stir-fry 1 minute. Stir in salad dressing, pepper and Italian herb blend.

4. Add spaghetti and toss until well-combined and heated through. To serve, sprinkle with grated Parmesan cheese.

Calories per serving:	622
Grams of fat:	30.6
Percentage fat calories:	44%
Cholesterol:	4 mg.

Chickpea Pasta Platter With Rosemary

Serves 4 to 6

Prep Time: 10 minutes
Cooking Time: 15 minutes

1   pound whole wheat, artichoke or other pasta

3   tablespoons olive oil

2   cups cooked chickpeas

2   fresh tomatoes, peeled, seeded and chopped

1   tablespoon fresh rosemary sprigs, plus extra for garnish

    Freshly ground black pepper to taste

Simple, satisfying and ready in minutes — if you cook the chickpeas ahead of time or buy them already cooked in cans or jars. One cup of dry chickpeas cooked for 3 hours in 4 cups of water yields 4 cups of cooked beans. If fresh tomatoes aren't available, substitute natural pasta sauce.

1. Cook pasta 15 minutes or until firm but still tender. Drain and toss with 1 tablespoon olive oil.

2. Place pasta on a serving platter. Combine remaining olive oil, tomatoes, chickpeas and rosemary and spoon over pasta. Grind fresh black pepper on top and garnish with rosemary sprigs. Serve warm or at room temperature.

Calories per serving:	*667*
Grams of fat:	*15*
Percentage fat calories:	*20%*
Cholesterol:	*0 mg.*

Pesto Spaghetti Squash With Broccoli

Serves 2 to 4

Prep Time: 15 minutes

1   large spaghetti squash

1   package pesto mix,
     prepared according to
     directions, or 1 small jar
     prepared pesto

2   tablespoons pine nuts

1   cup steamed broccoli
     florets

You may have seen hefty yellow spaghetti squash in the produce section and wondered what to do with it. When the squash is cooked and halved, the center can be scraped with a fork to produce spaghettilike strands. They make a low-calorie, low-carbohydrate alternative to pasta and provide significant amounts of vitamin A.

1. To cook spaghetti squash, cut in half and steam 15 to 20 minutes or place squash cut side down on a baking sheet and bake 20 minutes at 350°F.

2. While squash is still hot, remove spaghetti strands and set aside hollow squash shells. Toss spaghetti with pesto and pine nuts. Add broccoli and continue tossing to coat with pesto.

3. Serve spaghetti in reserved squash shells.

Calories per serving:	*267*
Grams of fat:	*12*
Percentage fat calories:	*41%*
Cholesterol:	*0 mg.*

Garlic Honey Turkey Stir-Fry

Serves 6

Prep Time: 20 minutes
Cooking Time: 15 to 20 minutes

2   tablespoons vegetable oil

1½ pounds boneless, skinless
      turkey breast, cut into
      1-inch pieces

1   cooked acorn squash,
      peeled and cut into
      1-inch pieces

1   cup broccoli florets

1   cup brussels sprouts,
      separated into leaves

Sauce:

½   cup honey

3   minced garlic cloves

¼   cup ginger tamari sauce

2   tablespoons sesame oil

3   tablespoons umeboshi
      paste

1   tablespoon hot pepper
      sauce

      Chopped scallions for
      garnish

In this colorful and satisfying dish, tempeh or tofu may be substituted for the turkey. Bake halved, seeded acorn squash cut side down at 350°F for 30 minutes. It should be slightly firm, as it will be stir-fried for a few minutes.

1. Heat oil in a large skillet or wok over moderate heat. Add turkey and cook, stirring, for 5 to 8 minutes until just cooked through. Take care not to overcook, which toughens turkey.

2. Transfer turkey to a covered bowl. Add broccoli, brussels sprouts and squash to the skillet and cook over moderately high heat, stirring, until broccoli is bright green and tender but still firm, about 5 minutes. Add vegetables to the turkey.

3. Combine honey, garlic, tamari, sesame oil, umeboshi paste and hot sauce, then add to the skillet and heat, stirring. Return turkey and vegetables to the skillet and toss to coat with sauce. Garnish with chopped scallions and serve.

Calories per serving:	415
Grams of fat:	13.6
Percentage fat calories:	29%
Cholesterol:	86 mg.

Tangy Tandoori Bake

Serves 4

Prep Time: 12 minutes
Cooking Time: 25 minutes

2 boneless, skinless chicken breasts, halved, or one 8-ounce package tempeh, cubed

¼ cup lemon juice

1 tablespoon tamari

2 tablespoons curry powder

1 tablespoon paprika

1 cup nonfat milk

1½ cups stock or water

¼ cup fresh cilantro, minced

½ cup nonfat plain yogurt

1 cup quick-cooking brown rice

This tasty tandoori-style casserole gets you out of the kitchen fast! Simply marinate chicken or tempeh in lemon juice, season with curry, toss over quick-cooking brown rice and bake.

1. Preheat oven to 375°F. In a shallow dish combine chicken or tempeh with tamari and lemon juice. Cover and marinate at least 10 minutes.

2. Combine spices with milk and water. Mix well. Spread rice evenly in an 8-inch pie pan. Arrange chicken or tempeh over rice and top with milk mixture.

3. Cover and bake 25 minutes or until liquid is absorbed and rice is tender. Stir in cilantro and transfer to a serving dish. Garnish with yogurt and additional paprika.

Calories per serving:	284
Grams of fat:	6
Percentage fat calories:	20%
Cholesterol:	84 mg.

Sizzling Shrimp Skewers

Serves 6

Prep Time: 15 minutes
Marinating Time: 4-6 hours
Cooking Time: 5 minutes

12 jumbo shrimp

½ cup pomegranate juice

2 cloves garlic

1 serrano pepper

½ cup red onion

2 tablespoons honey

¼ teaspoon sea salt

2 tablespoons lemon juice

1 green bell pepper

12 cherry tomatoes

The next time you barbecue, try these speedy kebabs and get ready for rave reviews.

1. Peel and devein shrimp, leaving tail section intact. Place in a shallow dish.

2. Combine pomegranate juice, garlic, serrano pepper, onion, honey, salt and lemon juice in a blender and puree. Pour over shrimp and marinate 4 to 6 hours.

3. Remove ribs and seeds from green pepper and cut into 1-inch pieces. Thread shrimp, peppers and tomatoes onto skewers. Cook over hot charcoal or under a broiler until shrimp are pink and juicy. Turn once during cooking.

Calories per serving:	73
Grams of fat:	.6
Percentage fat calories:	7%
Cholesterol:	22 mg.

Miso Fish Florentine

Serves 8

Prep Time: 20 minutes
Cooking Time: 5 minutes

2   pounds fresh or frozen
      fish fillets such as sole,
      haddock or flounder

2   large onions, sliced

3   tablespoons tamari

½   cup mellow miso

4   tablespoons water

1   teaspoon minced fresh
      ginger

3   scallion greens, thinly
      sliced

1   pound fresh spinach,
      washed and stemmed

2   carrots, julienned and
      steamed

1   large leek, julienned
      and steamed

Surprisingly simple to prepare, this savory fish dish will please everyone with its gentle flavor. Miso is such a nutritious, wholesome food that it makes sense to include it in recipes whenever possible.

1. Preheat the broiler. Spread onions in a glass baking dish. Cut fish into 8 equal-sized pieces and place on top of onions.

2. In a small bowl, combine tamari, miso, water and ginger to make a smooth paste. Spread evenly over fish.

3. Broil about 5 minutes until almost flaky but not dry. Meanwhile, steam spinach 1 minute, drain and place on a large serving platter. Arrange pieces of fish on the bed of spinach and surround with steamed leeks and carrots.

Calories per serving:	204
Grams of fat:	2.8
Percentage fat calories:	12%
Cholesterol:	54 mg.

Wasabi Fish With Vegetable Ribbons

Serves 2

Prep Time: 10 minutes
Cooking Time: 20 minutes

½   pound fish fillets such as sole, flounder or other firm fish

¼   cup cracker crumbs

1   medium carrot, julienned

1   medium zucchini or summer squash, julienned

1   teaspoon prepared wasabi

2   tablespoons nonfat plain yogurt

½   teaspoon hot pepper sesame oil

When time's of the essence, a package of natural frozen fillets or some fresh fish guarantees a quick, wholesome meal. We crisped the fish with cracker crumbs and baked it in a foil pouch with julienned vegetables, then spooned on a sauce of yogurt and wasabi, a hot Japanese mustard.

1.   Preheat oven to 350°F. Dredge fish fillets in cracker crumbs. Place in the center of a piece of aluminum foil.

2.   Place carrot and zucchini slivers on top of fish. Bring the edges of the foil together, then roll and fold to seal the package. Place on a cookie sheet on lowest oven rack and bake 20 minutes. Transfer to a plate to serve.

3.   To make sauce, mix wasabi, yogurt and sesame oil and spoon over fish.

Calories per serving:	223
Grams of fat:	2.3
Percentage fat calories:	9%
Cholesterol:	54 mg.

Fragrant Fish Fillets In Foil

Serves 4

Prep Time: 15 minutes
Cooking Time: 15 to 20 minutes

1   pound firm white fish
    fillets
1   lime, sliced
1   small onion, thinly sliced
1   teaspoon oregano
    Dash of cumin
1   garlic clove, minced
    Fresh cilantro

Frozen fish fillets are great for fast meals because they thaw quickly and can be cooked frozen in a pinch, especially when this simple method is employed. An added benefit is that there's no pan to clean up later! The aroma when you open the foil is absolutely mouthwatering.

1. Place fish fillets in a square of double-thickness or heavy-duty foil. Arrange lime and onion over the fish, drizzle with olive oil and sprinkle with seasonings.

2. Fold up the edges of the foil and seal to make an airtight package. Place over hot coals and grill 15 to 20 minutes.

Calories per serving:	139
Grams of fat:	1.5
Percentage fat calories:	10%
Cholesterol:	54 mg.

Miso Grilled Fish

Serves 6

Prep Time: 5 minutes
Grilling Time: 12 minutes

¼   cup mellow miso

4   pounds fresh fish fillets,
    1-inch thick

1   medium onion, sliced

Some fish such as bluefish, halibut, salmon or swordfish are easier to grill because they resist falling apart when turned. Fish cooks quickly on the grill and should take no longer than 10 to 12 minutes. To test the coals, hold the palm of your hand at the approximate cooking level, about 5 inches above the coals. If you can hold your palm steady for only 3 seconds, the coals are perfect.

1. Combine miso and 2 to 3 tablespoons water to a catsuplike consistency. Baste fish with miso mixture, top with sliced onions and transfer to the grill. Cook approximately 7 minutes. Turn, baste again and grill until fish flakes easily.

Calories per serving:	318
Grams of fat:	4.4
Percentage fat calories:	12%
Cholesterol:	145 mg.

Miso-Marinated Tofu & Cherry Tomato Kebabs

Serves 6

Prep Time: 15 minutes
Marinating Time: 1 hour
Cooking Time: 10 to 15 minutes

1   5-ounce bottle barbecue
    sauce

1   tablespoon mellow miso

1½ pounds firm tofu, cut
    into cubes slightly
    smaller than the cherry
    tomatoes

1   pint cherry tomatoes

Miso, that great multipurpose soyfood, is perfect for marinades. When used in moderate amounts, it lends a pleasant savory flavor to all sorts of barbecue sauces.

1. In a medium bowl, combine barbecue sauce and miso. Add tofu cubes and marinate at least an hour, turning occasionally.

2. To grill, alternate tofu cubes and cherry tomatoes on greased bamboo or metal skewers. Grill over hot coals 10 to 15 minutes, turning occasionally.

Calories per serving:	151
Grams of fat:	8
Percentage fat calories:	48%
Cholesterol:	0 mg.

Delicious! Marinades

Try one of our Delicious! marinades the next time you barbecue or broil.

TRY	MADE FROM	FOR MARINATING
SWEET 'N SOUR SESAME	2 Tbl. miso, 1 Tbl. honey, 2 tsp. each minced garlic and ginger, 1 tsp. toasted sesame oil.	Tofu, chicken, tempeh
VERY BERRY SURPRISE	¼ cup raspberry vinegar, 2 Tbl. canola oil, ¼ cup fresh mint, salt and pepper to taste, ¼ cup plain yogurt, ⅓ cup raspberries.	Chicken breasts, tempeh, salmon, tuna
FESTIVE FAJITA	½ cup lime juice, ¼ cup oil, 1 sliced onion, 1 Tbl. minced garlic, ¼ cup cilantro, 1 sliced jalapeño pepper, 1 diced red pepper, salt and pepper to taste.	Seafood, chicken breasts, tofu, tempeh
SPARKLING BOMBAY BLEND	½ cup sparkling cider, 1 sliced onion, 1 cup plain yogurt, 3 Tbl. honey, 1 Tbl. curry powder, salt and pepper to taste.	Vegetables, chicken, shrimp
YUMMY UME	¼ cup umeboshi plum vinegar, 1 tsp. minced garlic, 3 Tbl. tarragon, ¼ cup oil, 1 tsp. hot pepper flakes, 2 Tbl. tamari.	Tofu, tempeh, eggplant, scallops
CAJUN BAR-B-Q SAUCE	¼ cup cider vinegar, ½ cup catsup, 3 Tbl. Cajun spice blend, 1 sliced onion, ¼ cup parsley, 3 Tbl. maple syrup, black and cayenne pepper to taste.	Chicken, seafood, tempeh
CHINESE FIVE SPICE	⅓ cup tamari, 1 Tbl. garlic, 2 Tbl. lemon juice, 2 tsp. mirin, 2 tsp. Chinese five spice blend.	Seafood, tempeh, tofu, vegetables
PRESTO PESTO	¼ cup balsamic vinegar, ½ cup basil, ¼ cup olive oil, 3 Tbl. garlic, ½ cup Parmesan cheese.	Seafood, chicken, tofu, vegetables, tempeh
HOT 'N SPICY	1 cup red salsa, 1 sliced onion, ¼ cup cilantro, 2 tsp. cumin, 3 Tbl. oil.	Tofu, vegetables, chicken

Barbecued Tofu & Vegetables

Serves 4

Prep Time: 10 minutes
Grilling Time: 20 minutes

4   **ears of fresh corn, husks and silk intact**

1   **pound firm tofu, sliced thickly**

2   **medium zucchini or summer squash, halved**

1   **large onion, sliced**

1   **cup barbecue sauce**

Use only very firm tofu on the grill. Wrap the block of tofu in cheesecloth or a linen dishcloth and place a plate or cutting board on top to squeeze out the excess moisture. (Or use frozen tofu that has thawed in the refrigerator.) If you like a stronger barbecued flavor, marinate the tofu in the sauce a few hours before grilling. Be sure to slice it fairly thick so that it holds up for grilling. If you use aluminum foil on the grill, brush a little oil on it so the tofu doesn't stick.

1. Soak corn in salted water 10 to 20 minutes before placing it on the grill. Rotate corn frequently until husks are uniformly charred.

2. After putting corn on the grill, add sliced tofu, squash and onions. Baste frequently with barbecue sauce. After about 8 minutes, turn and baste again.

3. The corn is done when kernels emit water after being pierced with a sharp knife. The other vegetables are ready when a knife slides in easily. Husk corn before serving. Serve grilled tofu and vegetables with additional barbecue sauce.

Calories per serving:	*307*
Grams of fat:	*11*
Percentage fat calories:	*33%*
Cholesterol:	*0 mg.*

Royal Tofu Roulade

Serves 6 to 8

Prep Time: 1 hour
Freezing Time: 2 hours
Cooking Time: 1 hour

2½ **pounds firm tofu**

½ **cup tamari**

2 **egg whites**

1 **teaspoon curry powder**

1 **teaspoon rosemary**

1 **teaspoon sage**

1 **teaspoon thyme**

1 **teaspoon garlic powder**

½ **teaspoon sea salt**

¼ **teaspoon black pepper**

Dash Tabasco sauce

Olive oil or cooking spray

This delectable stuffed delight takes tofu to new culinary heights.

1. Blend tofu with egg whites and spices in a food processor until completely smooth.

2. Cover a medium-sized cookie sheet (9- x 14-inch) with foil and oil lightly with olive oil or cooking spray.

3. Pour tofu mixture onto the cookie sheet and spread evenly in a layer about ¼-inch thick. While spreading, press tofu into the cookie sheet to smooth out any air pockets and creases. Cover with plastic wrap and place in the freezer for 2 hours until completely frozen.

4. Preheat oven to 350°F.

5. Remove plastic covering from tofu and place the cookie sheet directly into the oven. Bake 1 hour until a golden brown skin forms on the underside.

6. Remove from oven and cool 30 minutes.

7. Stuff roulade with Wild Rice Stuffing (page 146) and serve with Crimson Cranberry Glaze (page 188).

Calories per serving:	580
Grams of fat:	15
Percentage fat calories:	25%
Cholesterol:	0 mg.

How To Stuff The Roulade

1. After roulade has cooled 30 minutes, carefully turn the whole tofu sheet onto a large piece of cheesecloth or thin towel so the underside is on top.

2. Using the cloth as a support to lift and maneuver the roulade, slide $\frac{1}{3}$ of the longer end of the roulade onto a serving plate with baked underside still facing up. The edge of the tofu sheet should be covering $\frac{3}{4}$ of the plate.

3. Hold the other $\frac{2}{3}$ of the tofu sheet up and have a helper spoon 6 cups of stuffing on top of plated portion of the roulade.

4. Form stuffing into a cylinder that the remaining tofu sheet can easily roll around.

5. Tuck the second end underneath and bring ends together. Gently pack in more stuffing from both ends.

6. Helpful hints: If roulade begins to split, reposition it so the split area is underneath on the plate. If you need to trim the roulade, extra pieces can be served on the side or used for sandwiches.

Wild Rice Stuffing

Serves 6 to 8 portions for the Tofu Roulade with extra

Prep Time: 40 minutes
Cooking Time: 1 hour

1	pound (4 cups) raw wild rice
1	10-ounce package soy sausage, sliced
1½	ounces dried shiitake mushrooms
1	cup herb stuffing mix
1	cup onions, minced
8	cloves fresh garlic, minced
2	ounces dried cherries
1	tablespoon dried rosemary
1	tablespoon dried thyme
1	tablespoon dried sage
1	tablespoon dried savory
1	teaspoon celery seed
1	tablespoon sea salt
½	teaspoon black pepper
¼	cup fresh parsley, minced

The soy sausage flavor brings out the best in this savory stuffing.

1. Boil 8 cups water in a 4-quart saucepan. Add wild rice and bring to a boil, then lower heat and simmer rice 40 minutes. The rice is done when it's soft and the liquid has been absorbed. Drain excess water and set aside.

2. Soak mushrooms in 2 cups warm water for 20 minutes. When soft, drain liquid and save. Slice mushrooms thinly.

3. In a large, nonstick frying pan, sauté onions, garlic, soy sausage and mushrooms until onions are translucent. Add spices and herbs.

4. Add mushroom liquid and cherries, then bring to a boil.

5. Add stuffing mix and rice. Stir well. Cook on low heat 3 to 4 minutes until liquid is absorbed.

Tofu Spinach Torte

Serves 8

Prep Time: 20 minutes
Cooking Time: 25 minutes

2   10-ounce packages frozen chopped spinach

2   cups cornbread dressing mix

1½ cups water

2   cloves garlic

1   cup diced onion

½   cup diced celery

4   ounces soft tofu, drained

1   tablespoon poultry seasoning

     Sea salt and black pepper to taste

2   pounds firm tofu

For an elegant main dish, drench this torte with tomato or pesto sauce. Or skip the sauce and serve it alongside a traditional turkey dinner.

1. Thaw spinach completely and squeeze in a clean kitchen towel to remove as much liquid as possible. Combine with dressing and water and stir to mix.

2. Sauté garlic, onion and celery in ¼ cup water until vegetables are wilted. Add to spinach. Beat soft tofu until smooth and stir into spinach mixture along with seasonings.

3. Slice firm tofu into ½-inch-thick pieces. Line bottom and sides of a nonstick loaf pan or heat-proof bowl with ¾ of the tofu. Fill mold with layers of spinach and tofu, ending with tofu. (Steps 1 through 3 may be prepared up to 24 hours in advance.)

4. Place mold on a rack in a large pot or Oriental steamer. Cover and steam 30 minutes. Remove from heat and cool 5 minutes. With a paring knife, loosen tofu from sides of mold and invert onto a serving plate.

Calories per serving:	*180*
Grams of fat:	*7*
Percentage fat calories:	*35%*
Cholesterol:	*0 mg.*

Tempeh & Red Peppers With Udon

Serves 4

Prep Time: 15 minutes
Cooking Time: 20 minutes

1   large onion, chopped

1-2 cloves garlic, minced

1-2 teaspoons olive oil

½   teaspoon oregano

½   teaspoon thyme

1   large carrot, julienned

1   red bell pepper, cut in thin strips

1   package tempeh, cut in half lengthwise, then in strips

4   tablespoons arrowroot

2   tablespoons mirin

3   tablespoons tamari

1   cup water

½   cup chopped parsley

Udon Noodles:

1   8-ounce package udon noodles

½   teaspoon sesame oil

   Pinch of sea salt

This colorful, nutritious meal is very satisfying when served over udon noodles or grains.

1. Sauté onion, garlic and herbs in oil in a large skillet until onion softens. Add tempeh, carrots, then pepper, letting each cook a few minutes before adding the next. When tempeh starts to get a little golden, add arrowroot, coating ingredients well.

2. Mix mirin, tamari and 1 cup water together and add slowly, stirring as you go. This makes a nice gravy. Let it simmer on low heat 15 to 20 minutes. Serve over udon noodles garnished with parsley.

3. To prepare udon noodles, add sesame oil and a pinch of salt to a pot of boiling water. Drop in noodles. Let water come to a boil again. Add enough cold water to stop boiling. Bring to a boil again. Repeat. When water boils a third time, test noodles to make sure they're done.

Calories per serving:	*424*
Grams of fat:	*4.8*
Percentage fat calories:	*10%*
Cholesterol:	*0 mg.*

Tempeh Tahiti

Serves 4 to 6

Prep Time: 15 minutes
Cooking Time: 20 minutes

1	cup barbecue sauce
1½	cups water
1	teaspoon minced ginger
1	garlic clove, minced
1	cup pineapple chunks
1	medium red bell pepper, seeded and chopped
2	celery stalks, sliced
1	pound tempeh, cubed
1	cup snow peas
3	cups cooked brown rice

Tempeh, an extremely nutritious soyfood, is also rich in fiber and easy to digest, an aid to those trying to lose weight. It's chewy and satisfying, too. It can be steamed or simmered gently for about 10 minutes. Salt-free and high in vitamin B-12, this Indonesian food has become popular in this country.

1. In a large saucepan, combine barbecue sauce, 1½ cups water, ginger, garlic, pineapple, pepper and celery and simmer over moderate heat until pepper and celery are tender but still crisp, about 5 minutes.

2. Add tempeh and cook 10 minutes longer. Add snow peas and cook just until bright green, less than 5 minutes. Serve over cooked brown rice.

Calories per serving:	*330*
Grams of fat:	*6.2*
Percentage fat calories:	*17%*
Cholesterol:	*0 mg.*

Tempura Temptation

Serves 6

Prep Time: 15 minutes
Cooking Time: 15 minutes

5   rice cakes

2   egg whites

1   tablespoon sesame oil

¼   pound mushrooms

2   carrots, sliced and steamed

1   zucchini, sliced

1   red bell pepper, sliced

Try this twist on traditional tempura. Coat vegetables with crumbled rice cakes then pop them in the oven for a taste-tempting treat!

1. Preheat oven to 425°F. Lightly brush a baking sheet with oil. Break rice cakes into pieces and crush finely in a food processor or blender.

2. Beat egg whites until frothy. Dip vegetable pieces into egg whites, then roll in rice cakes to coat. Place on baking sheet and bake until lightly browned, about 15 minutes.

3. Serve with soy sauce or other Oriental dipping sauce.

Calories per serving:	90
Grams of fat:	2.6
Percentage fat calories:	26%
Cholesterol:	0 mg.

Nori Roll-Ups

Serves 8

Prep Time: 20 minutes
Cooking Time: 20 minutes

1   cup raw sushi rice

1¼   cups water

3   tablespoons rice vinegar

2   teaspoons mirin

4   sheets sushi nori

1   cup mixed vegetables
        (snow peas, sprouts,
        sliced carrots,
        cucumbers)

1   tablespoon wasabi
        powder

½   cup tamari

Sheets of nori make delicious fun-filled treats filled with glistening sushi rice and a colorful mixture of vegetables. Add wasabi and you're ready to roll!

1. Rinse rice in cold water. Put in a heavy saucepan with water, cover and bring to a boil. Reduce heat and simmer 15 minutes or until all water is absorbed. Remove from heat and set aside, covered, for 20 minutes.

2. Heat vinegar and mirin. Pour over rice and stir until rice glistens.

3. To assemble, cut sheets of nori into triangles. Place one triangle on a dry surface with the wide apex away from you and the long side on your right. Pat a layer of rice over right half of the sheet, dampening your fingertips with water to prevent rice from sticking.

4. Arrange 10 to 12 slices of vegetables along left edge of the rice.

5. Bring tip of long side of nori to tip of wide apex. Roll nori into a cone shape. Seal shut with cold water. Repeat with remaining nori and vegetables.

6. Mix wasabi with enough hot water to form a thick paste. Serve roll-ups with wasabi and tamari.

Calories per serving:	92
Grams of fat:	.2
Percentage fat calories:	2%
Cholesterol:	0 mg.

Oriental Bean Cakes

Yields 10 patties

Prep Time: 15 minutes
Cooking Time: 35 minutes

1 cup dried adzuki beans

½ cup raw brown rice

3½ cups water

1 tablespoon Chinese five spice powder

1 teaspoon ginger, minced

2 tablespoons tamari

1 teaspoon cayenne pepper

½ cup scallions, minced

½ cup unseasoned whole wheat bread crumbs

1 red bell pepper, diced

2 tablespoons sesame seeds

These burgers are good on toasted rice cakes with sweet-and-sour sauce and a side of stir-fried vegetables.

1. Pick over beans and rice and rinse well. Combine in pressure cooker with water, 1 teaspoon five spice powder and ginger. Bring to a boil and skim foam that rises to surface. Remove from heat and secure cooker top in place. Return to heat and bring to high pressure. Cook 20 minutes.

2. Place cooker in sink and run cold water over top to release pressure. Remove lid and stir in remaining five spice powder, tamari, cayenne, scallions, bread crumbs and pepper.

3. When cool enough to handle, form into patties. Sprinkle sesame seeds over top and place on nonstick baking sheet.

4. Preheat oven to 350°F. Bake cakes until hot in the center, about 15 minutes.

Note: *To make Oriental Bean Cakes in a hurry, skip Step 1 and add seasonings and bread crumbs to 2 cups canned adzuki beans and 1½ cups prepared quick-cooking brown rice. Proceed with Step 3.*

Calories per serving:	*111*
Grams of fat:	*1.8*
Percentage fat calories:	*14%*
Cholesterol:	*0 mg.*

Protein-Packed Indian Pancakes (Dosas)

Serves 8

Prep Time: 10 minutes
Cooking Time: 20 minutes

1   cup nonfat plain yogurt

1   teaspoon baking soda

1½ cups chickpea flour or
    instant hummus mix

1½ cups rice flour

½   teaspoon sea salt

2   cups water

4   tablespoons ghee or
    vegetable oil

In India, "dosas" are made by fermenting raw rice and dried beans. In our version, chickpea and rice flour speed up the process.

1. In a bowl, stir together yogurt and baking soda. The mixture should bubble and increase in volume.

2. Combine flours and salt in a food processor. With motor running, add water and yogurt mixture and process until smooth. Set aside 10 minutes.

3. Brush a 10-inch nonstick skillet with ghee and place over medium heat until water dances on its surface. Ladle ⅓ cup batter into center of the pan. After a few seconds, spread batter into an 8-inch pancake. Drizzle 1 teaspoon ghee over the surface and around the edge of the dosa. Cook 3 minutes or until top is bubbly and bottom is lightly browned. Using a spatula, loosen the edge of the dosa as it cooks. Flip and cook briefly on the other side, then flip again and transfer to a plate. Place in a warm oven while cooking remaining batter.

4. To serve, top bubbly side of dosa with curried vegetables or spread with a thin layer of chutney. Roll pancake around filling and transfer to a serving plate.

Calories per serving:	*283*
Grams of fat:	*10*
Percentage fat calories:	*31%*
Cholesterol:	*0 mg.*

Hurry-Curry Vegetables

Serves 8

Prep Time: 15 minutes
Cooking Time: 15 minutes

1   onion, diced

1   tablespoon peanut oil

3   red potatoes, diced

2   carrots, diced

1   cup cauliflower pieces

3½ tablespoons curry powder

¼   teaspoon sea salt or tamari

1¼ cups water

1   green or red bell pepper, diced

1   cup frozen peas, thawed

¼   cup fresh cilantro, minced

For a special treat, serve this curry dish over basmati rice or wrap it in crispy Protein-Packed Indian Pancakes (page 153).

1. In a large skillet, sauté onion in oil over medium heat until wilted. Add potatoes, carrots, cauliflower, curry powder, salt or tamari, water and mix well. Reduce heat to low. Cover and simmer, stirring occasionally until potatoes are tender.

2. Turn heat to medium and add pepper. Cook 5 minutes or until pepper begins to soften. Stir in peas and cilantro and warm through. Adjust seasonings.

Calories per serving:	*102*
Grams of fat:	*2.3*
Percentage fat calories:	*20%*
Cholesterol:	*0 mg.*

Blazing Yellow Squash

Serves 6

Prep Time: 15 minutes
Cooking Time: 20 minutes

2   tablespoons vegetable oil

1   medium onion, chopped

2   garlic cloves, minced

½   teaspoon minced fresh ginger

½   teaspoon red pepper flakes

¼   teaspoon turmeric

1   tablespoon peach preserves

1   pound butternut squash, peeled and cut into ½-inch cubes

A glorious way to serve naturally sweet butternut or acorn squash, this Indian dish makes an exciting yet simple meal with brown rice and a side dish of sliced cucumbers in plain yogurt.

1. Sauté onion and garlic in vegetable oil until soft. Stir in ginger, hot pepper, turmeric, preserves and ½ cup water.

2. Add squash cubes and cook, stirring, for 5 minutes. Cover, reduce heat to low and cook 10 minutes longer until squash is soft but still firm.

Calories per serving:	98
Grams of fat:	3
Percentage fat calories:	29%
Cholesterol:	0 mg.

Tic-Tac-Tortilla Stacks

Serves 6

Prep Time: 15 minutes
Cooking Time: 10 minutes

3   15-ounce cans bean chili

12   corn tortillas or whole wheat chapatis

1   cup shredded lettuce

1   cup salsa

1   package instant refried beans, prepared according to label directions

3   tablespoons chopped fresh cilantro or parsley

1   cup plain nonfat yogurt, drained

   Scallion greens, black olives, grated carrot and slices of red bell pepper and tomato for garnish

Mexican-style food is always a great favorite, and this easy-to-prepare dish illustrates how natural convenience foods can add spicy interest to the simplest meals.

1.   Heat chili in a saucepan until warmed through. Wrap tortillas in foil and heat in oven.

2.   To make each stack, place a tortilla on a plate. Top with some lettuce and salsa and another tortilla. Spread with refried beans and cilantro and top with another tortilla. Spread with yogurt and top with another tortilla. Top with chili and another tortilla. Repeat with remaining ingredients.

3.   To garnish, divide the top of each stack into segments with scallion greens and decorate as desired with sliced olives, grated carrot, peppers and tomatoes.

Calories per serving:	887
Grams of fat:	1.6
Percentage fat calories:	2%
Cholesterol:	0 mg.

Fiery Tofu Fajitas

Serves 6

Prep Time: 15 minutes
Marinating Time: 4 hours
Cooking Time: 10 minutes

1	pound firm tofu
1	red bell pepper, sliced
1	green bell pepper, sliced
1	jalapeño pepper, minced
1	red onion, sliced
½	package dry Italian salad dressing mix
¾	cup water
⅓	cup lemon juice
2	cloves garlic, sliced
1	tablespoon vegetable oil
2	teaspoons tamari
6	whole wheat tortillas
	Avocado slices and black olives for garnish

For a simple fajita-style marinade, combine tofu with dry salad dressing mix, lemon juice and slivers of bell pepper. The mixture can be prepared up to a day in advance.

1. Drain tofu and cut into small cubes. Combine with peppers and onion in a shallow dish.

2. Combine remaining ingredients, except tortillas, and pour over tofu. Stir to mix. Marinate at least 4 hours.

3. Cook in a skillet over charcoal or broil until peppers are soft, about 10 minutes.

4. Wrap fajita mixture in tortillas to serve. Garnish with avocado slices and black olives.

Calories per serving:	*247*
Grams of fat:	*10.5*
Percentage fat calories:	*38%*
Cholesterol:	*0 mg.*

Warming Winter Chili

Serves 8

Prep Time: 15 minutes
Cooking Time: 45 minutes

1½ cups diced onion

3   cloves garlic, minced

1½ cups salsa

2   teaspoons cumin

2   teaspoons chili powder

4   cups tomato juice

½   cup diced green bell
pepper

1½ cups cooked black beans

1½ cups cooked kidney
beans

¾   cup Textured
Vegetable Protein

⅓   cup minced fresh
cilantro

¼   cup corn kernels

Sea salt and black
pepper to taste

Imagine homemade chili in less than an hour! This quick and simple chili gets its flavorful flair from fresh cilantro and its meaty texture from Textured Vegetable Protein.

1. In a large saucepan, combine onions, garlic, salsa, cumin, chili powder and juice. Simmer 10 minutes until onions are tender. Add green pepper and beans, cover and simmer another 15 minutes.

2. Stir in Textured Vegetable Protein. Continue to simmer, stirring frequently until tender, about 15 minutes. Add cilantro and corn. Season to taste with salt and pepper.

Calories per serving:	164
Grams of fat:	.8
Percentage fat calories:	4%
Cholesterol:	0 mg.

Herbed Lentil & Potato Stew

Serves 4

Prep Time: 10 to 15 minutes
Cooking Time: 40 minutes

1   onion, chopped

1   clove garlic, minced

1   teaspoon olive oil

1   teaspoon marjoram

1   teaspoon rosemary

1   teaspoon thyme

1   large or 2 small potatoes, cubed

1   cup brown lentils, picked over and rinsed

1   4-inch strip kombu, soaked in water 5 minutes

4   cups stock or water

    Sea salt

When fall evenings turn chilly, make a batch of this hearty stew for a quick, nutritious meal.

1. Sauté onion and garlic in olive oil in a soup pot. When onion is soft, add herbs. Add potatoes, lentils, kombu and stock or water. Bring to a boil. Lower heat and simmer 1 hour, covered. Or use a pressure cooker (this gives the soup a creamier texture); bring to pressure and let simmer 40 minutes.

2. Remove kombu after cooking and add salt to taste.

Calories per serving:	249
Grams of fat:	2
Percentage fat calories:	7%
Cholesterol:	0 mg.

Neapolitan Polenta Pie

Serves 8

Prep Time: 20 minutes
Draining Time: 10 hours
Cooking Time: 35 minutes

12   ounces nonfat plain
     yogurt

1   cup polenta

3   cups water

1   teaspoon sea salt

1½ cups pizza sauce

1   cup red onion, sliced

¼   pound field mushrooms,
     sliced

2   ounces dried porcini
     mushrooms, soaked

3   tablespoons capers

1   tomato, sliced

1   cup green bell pepper,
     sliced

3   tablespoons Parmesan
     cheese, grated

⅓   cup fresh basil, chopped

A unique blend of flavors and textures highlights this layered pie. Try it when you're in the mood for a hearty, stick-to-the-ribs dish.

1. The day before serving, prepare "cheese" from yogurt by mixing yogurt with ½ teaspoon salt and placing in a strainer lined with several layers of cheesecloth. Squeeze cloth very gently around yogurt and place over bowl. Refrigerate and drain for at least 10 hours. Before continuing with recipe, carefully remove cheesecloth from ball of cheese.

2. Stir polenta into boiling water. Add ½ teaspoon salt. Cover and cook over low heat, stirring frequently, for 15 minutes or until thick and soft. Pour into a 9-inch nonstick pie plate and spread evenly over bottom and sides.

3. Preheat oven to 425°F. Spread pizza sauce over polenta. Arrange vegetables over sauce, top with yogurt cheese, capers and Parmesan cheese. Bake 25 minutes or until pie is bubbling hot throughout. Remove from oven and top with basil.

Calories per serving:	147
Grams of fat:	1.8
Percentage fat calories:	11%
Cholesterol:	0 mg.

Couscous Primavera

Serves 3 to 4

Prep Time: 10 minutes
Cooking Time: 10 minutes

3	tablespoons vegetable oil
1	medium yellow bell pepper, chopped
1	medium zucchini, sliced
½	cup thinly sliced Bermuda onion
8	asparagus stalks
1	cup whole wheat couscous

If you've never tried couscous, the traditional grain dish of North Africa, you'll be pleasantly surprised by its sweet, light taste — a perfect foil for crunchy, springtime vegetables and a lively parsley sauce. Use any combination of vegetables desired, but be sure to take advantage of seasonal favorites, like asparagus.

1. In a medium skillet, heat 1 tablespoon oil over moderate heat. Add pepper, zucchini, onion and asparagus and sauté, stirring, for 5 minutes or until crisp-tender.

2. In a medium saucepan, bring 1¼ cups water to a boil. Add remaining oil and couscous. Cover, remove from heat and let stand 5 minutes.

3. Spoon couscous onto a serving platter and arrange vegetables on top.

Calories per serving:	371
Grams of fat:	16.3
Percentage fat calories:	40%
Cholesterol:	0 mg.

Tomato-Couscous Ring With Vegetables

Serves 8

Prep Time: 20 minutes
Chilling Time: 1 hour
Cooking Time: 10 minutes

2   cups whole wheat couscous

1½ tablespoons vegetable oil

2   cups pasta sauce

1   cup salsa

½ medium onion, chopped

3   cups lightly steamed vegetables (broccoli, cauliflower, carrots, etc.)

This is one of our most requested Delicious! *recipes. It's appropriate for a weekday meal but can also be the main dish for a dinner party.*

1. In a large saucepan, bring 4 cups water to a boil. Stir in couscous and oil, cover and remove from heat. After 10 minutes, stir again to fluff.

2. Add pasta sauce and salsa to couscous and mix well. Place in a lightly greased ring mold and refrigerate at least 1 hour.

3. To serve, unmold on a serving plate and fill with vegetables.

Calories per serving:	227
Grams of fat:	4.7
Percentage fat calories:	19%
Cholesterol:	0 mg.

Hot Tabouli To Go!

Serves 4

Prep Time: 10 minutes
Cooking Time: 2 hours

1   cup bulgur

¼   cup frozen peas

¼   cup chopped mint

4   scallions, minced

½   cucumber, seeded and
     diced

1   2-ounce jar pimientos

1¾   cup spicy tomato juice

This recipe is perfect for mornings when you're short on time. Just pour the ingredients into a thermos and you've got a hot lunch to go.

1. Place bulgur in a strainer and rinse with cold water. Transfer to a thermos. Add remaining ingredients except juice.

2. Heat juice to a boil. Pour into thermos and stir to combine. Seal thermos lid and let stand 2 to 8 hours, shaking thermos occasionally to mix salad.

Calories per serving:	*161*
Grams of fat:	*.6*
Percentage fat calories:	*3%*
Cholesterol:	*0 mg.*

Two-Step Stuffed Squash

Serves 8

Prep Time: 10 minutes
Cooking Time: 55 minutes

2   acorn squash

1   box tabouli mix

1½   cups water

1   apple, diced

1   tablespoon curry powder,
      or to taste

1   cup nonfat plain yogurt

⅓   cup raisins

¼   cup chopped cashews

      Sea salt and black pepper
      to taste

Add cooked shrimp or tofu to this hearty side dish and you'll have a satisfying main course.

1. Preheat oven to 400°F. Cut squash in half lengthwise. Scoop out and discard seeds. Season squash with salt and pepper. Cover and bake until soft, about 45 minutes.

2. Combine remaining ingredients. Mix well and set aside. When squash is cooked, fill with tabouli mixture. Cover and return to oven 10 minutes or until warmed through.

Calories per serving:	*228*
Grams of fat:	*3*
Percentage fat calories:	*12%*
Cholesterol:	*0 mg.*

Zucchini Earthburgers With Spring Onion Sauce

Serves 6

Prep Time: 10 minutes
Cooking Time: 15 minutes

1   10-ounce box grain burger mix

1   medium zucchini, julienned

1   tablespoon vegetable oil

Sauce:

1   tablespoon vegetable oil

2   scallions, minced

1   garlic clove, minced

½   small carrot, grated

¼   teaspoon each chili powder and paprika

1   10-ounce cake soft tofu

The fringe of fresh zucchini slivers on these crusty grain burgers makes them extra moist and appealing. They're terrific on seeded whole wheat buns with Spring Onion Sauce. Tuck in slices of tomato, a few alfalfa sprouts and red onion, if you like.

1. In a medium bowl, combine burger mix with 1½ cups boiling water and let stand 10 minutes.

2. Combine burger mix with zucchini and form into patties about ¾-inch thick. Cook burgers in a nonstick skillet over moderate heat until lightly browned on both sides, about 15 minutes. Or bake in a 375°F oven on a lightly oiled cookie sheet.

3. To make Spring Onion Sauce, combine all ingredients in a blender or food processor (in batches, if necessary). Blend until smooth and creamy. Sauce may be stored in a covered bowl in the refrigerator up to a week.

Calories per serving:	*198*
Grams of fat:	*7.4*
Percentage fat calories:	*34%*
Cholesterol:	*0 mg.*

One Terrific Tofu Burger

Serves 6

Prep Time: 5 minutes
Cooking Time: 6 minutes

2   egg whites

1   pound firm tofu, drained
     and mashed

1   4.4-ounce package tofu
     burger mix

1   small clove of chopped
     fresh garlic or
     2 teaspoons garlic
     seasoning blend

1   tablespoon chopped fresh
     thyme or ½ teaspoon
     dried

Beaten egg whites help lighten the texture of this tofu burger, while a judicious dose of fresh herbs gives the burger mixture great character. Since tofu is now available in aseptic packages that require no refrigeration and have a shelf life of 6 months, you can mix up these palatable patties whenever the urge for a big, juicy burger arises.

1. In a large bowl, beat egg whites until stiff peaks form. Add remaining ingredients and mix to combine.

2. Preheat broiler. Shape burger mixture into patties ½- to 1-inch thick and place on a nonstick broiler pan.

3. Broil 3 minutes on each side until browned. Serve on a whole wheat bun with your favorite trimmings.

Calories per serving:	*140*
Grams of fat:	*5*
Percentage fat calories:	*32%*
Cholesterol:	*0 mg.*

The Greatest Italian Hero

Serves 8

Prep Time: 20 minutes

Bean Salad:

1   cup cooked kidney beans

1   cup black or green olives, sliced

2   small or 1 large can tuna

1   cup cooked chickpeas

¾   cup Caesar salad dressing

¼   cup fresh basil, chopped

Sandwich:

1   package whole-grain hot dog buns

   Romaine or red leaf lettuce for lining the bread

¼   pound skim milk mozzarella, sliced

2   medium tomatoes, sliced

1   large red onion, sliced

½   cup red bell pepper rings

Who says natural foods aren't fun? This breathtaking submarine sandwich is a crowd-pleasing blend of tuna and bean salad in a spicy dressing layered with skim milk mozzarella cheese and all the fixings. Use hot dog buns or check your natural foods store for loaves of whole-grain French or Italian bread. This is a great dish for picnics and parties.

1. In a large bowl, combine kidney beans, olives, tuna, chickpeas, salad dressing and basil, stirring until thoroughly mixed.

2. Place buns on a large serving platter. Layer with lettuce, mozzarella, tomatoes, bean salad, onion and peppers. Serve immediately.

Calories per serving:	386
Grams of fat:	16
Percentage fat calories:	37%
Cholesterol:	31 mg.

Mushroom-Parsley Pita Sandwiches

Serves 4

Prep Time: 15 minutes

2   cups sliced fresh mushrooms

¾   cup nonfat plain yogurt

1   red bell pepper, seeded and sliced

1   teaspoon tamari

¾   cup coarsely chopped fresh parsley

¼   cup toasted pine nuts

4   pita breads, halved

Low-calorie and full of refreshing taste, this recipe demonstrates the assertive role vitamin A-rich fresh parsley can play as a salad ingredient instead of a timid garnish.

1.   In a medium bowl, combine mushrooms, yogurt, pepper, tamari and parsley. Cover and chill until ready to serve.

2.   Fill pita halves with salad and sprinkle with pine nuts just before serving.

Calories per serving:	242
Grams of fat:	7.4
Percentage fat calories:	27%
Cholesterol:	0 mg.

Side Dishes

Show-Stopping Side Dishes

We often treat side dishes as obligatory accompaniments to entrees, but a well-chosen side dish can show off your culinary wizardry.

Here, we've assembled an entourage of side dishes guaranteed to steal the show. Our delightful Stuffed Miniature Harvest Pumpkins (page 175) and aristocratic Artichokes With Curry Lemon Sauce (page 171) are visually stunning side dishes that do more than play understudy to an entree. And like all of our side dishes, they weigh in very low on the fat scale.

Along with side dishes, we've included savory sauces, relishes and chutneys. A dab of our sweet-and-sour Corn Raisin Relish (page 186) or a drizzle of Emerald Cress Sauce (page 182) will dazzle your eye and add a flavorful dimension to your meal. Choose one that contrasts yet harmonizes with the accompanying course.

Relishes and chutneys, which are pickled fruits and vegetables spiked with exotic seasonings, are naturally low-fat. However, sauces usually have an oil or animal product for a base and are inherently high-fat and high-cholesterol. Here are a few *Delicious!* ideas for eliminating fat from your favorite sauce recipes:

- For a low-fat, no-cholesterol sauce base, use homemade vegetable broth or dissolve vegetable bouillon in water. Miso or tamari diluted with water also makes a flavorful background for sauces as does broth made from dried shiitake mushrooms or sea vegetables like wakame or kombu.

- Instead of flour or cornstarch, thicken sauces with arrowroot, kuzu powder (an extract of Japanese kudzu similar to cornstarch) or mashed potatoes.

- Season sauces generously with natural flavorings such as pureed vegetables, garlic, fresh and dried herbs, sun-dried tomatoes, and gomasio (ground sesame seeds mixed with sea salt).

Artichokes With Curry Lemon Sauce

Serves 4

Prep Time: 15 minutes
Cooking Time: 15 to 20 minutes

4   **medium artichokes**

1   **lemon, halved, plus 1 tablespoon fresh lemon juice**

⅔   **cup soy mayonnaise**

1   **cup plain soy milk**

1   **teaspoon curry powder, or more to taste**

     Sea salt and freshly ground black pepper to taste

Artichokes are an elegant addition to a leisurely meal when eaten slowly, one leaf at a time. For a tasty, low-fat alternative to Curry Lemon Sauce, dip artichoke leaves in tangy Cucumber Dill Dressing (page 184).

1. To cook artichokes, cut off stem and rub stem end with lemon juice. Drop artichokes into a pot of boiling water, squeeze in lemon and boil about 15 minutes until heart is tender when pierced with a fork. Drain and plunge into ice water and let cool. Drain and dry with a dish towel.

2. Meanwhile, mix soy mayonnaise with soy milk and beat until smooth. Stir in lemon juice and curry powder and refrigerate until ready to serve.

3. Before serving artichokes, spread apart leaves and scrape out fuzzy part of choke with a spoon. Spoon sauce over artichokes or serve sauce on the side for dipping.

Calories per serving, 1 artichoke:	60
with ¼ cup sauce:	223
Grams of fat, 1 artichoke:	.2
with ¼ cup sauce:	17.5
Percentage fat calories, 1 artichoke:	3%
with ¼ cup sauce:	71%
Cholesterol, 1 artichoke:	0 mg.
with ¼ cup sauce:	0 mg.

Green Beans With Lemon & Wheat Germ

Serves 6

Prep Time: 10 minutes
Cooking Time: 5 minutes

2 pounds fresh green beans, trimmed

1 cup toasted wheat germ

Juice and zest of 1 large lemon

Sea salt and freshly ground black pepper to taste

The simple accent of fresh lemon juice and toasted wheat germ does wonderful things for lightly cooked green beans, as it would for steamed broccoli, cauliflower, carrots or other vegetables.

1. In a vegetable steamer or a colander set over a pan of boiling water, steam beans 5 minutes or until bright green and still crunchy. Drain and toss with wheat germ, lemon juice and zest, salt and pepper.

Calories per serving:	123
Grams of fat:	2.3
Percentage fat calories:	17%
Cholesterol:	0 mg.

Gingered Eggplant & Squash

Serves 4

Prep Time: 15 minutes
Cooking Time: 8 to 12 minutes

1   5-ounce bottle barbecue
     or teriyaki sauce

     Juice of 1 lemon

½   to 1 teaspoon minced
     ginger

1   teaspoon sesame seeds

1   large eggplant, sliced
     lengthwise

2   medium zucchini, cut
     into 1-inch pieces

Look for the youngest, smallest vegetables to use in this simple barbecue side dish. The pure flavors of yellow squash, zucchini, eggplant, bell peppers and even potatoes are enhanced by the zesty marinade and smoky flavor.

1. In a large bowl, combine barbecue or teriyaki sauce, lemon juice, ginger and sesame seeds. Add vegetables and toss to coat well.

2. Place squash and eggplant directly on a grill over hot coals. Grill, turning occasionally while basting with remaining sauce, 8 to 12 minutes until uniformly cooked.

Calories per serving:	119
Grams of fat:	3.2
Percentage fat calories:	24%
Cholesterol:	0 mg.

Summer Squash Rafts

Serves 2

Prep Time: 15 minutes
Cooking Time: 20 minutes

2   medium summer squash,
    halved lengthwise

¼   cup refried beans

¼   cup drained, crumbled
    feta cheese

¼   cup whole-grain stuffing
    mix

¼   cup chopped tomatoes

2   tablespoons salsa

When produce sections and farmers' markets yield piles of yellow and green summer squash, it's time to become inventive in the kitchen. Just make sure you have whole-grain stuffing mix, instant or prepared refried beans and salsa on hand. Other cheeses may be substituted for feta.

1. Preheat oven to 375°F. Steam squash for 5 minutes or microwave on medium power 2 minutes. Scoop out all but ¼-inch of the pulp. Turn squash upside down to drain.

2. Spread 1 tablespoon of refried beans in each squash half. Combine cheese and stuffing mix and distribute evenly in squash halves. Top with chopped tomatoes and salsa.

3. Bake 10 to 15 minutes until cheese is melted.

Calories per serving:	*115*
Grams of fat:	*3.6*
Percentage fat calories:	*28%*
Cholesterol:	*12 mg.*

Stuffed Miniature Harvest Pumpkins

Serves 8

Prep Time: 1 hour
Cooking Time: 1 hour

8	baby pumpkins
3	pounds fresh Swiss chard or spinach
4	shallots or 1 small onion, minced
4	tablespoons pastry flour
2	cups hot water
½	teaspoon sea salt
1	tablespoon mellow miso
⅛	teaspoon black pepper
⅛	teaspoon nutmeg

Bring the plentiful harvest to your table with colorful pumpkins. Your family will love these miniature gourds filled with healthy chard.

1. Preheat oven to 350°F. Wash and dry pumpkins. Carve a circle around the stem and remove the "lid" like a Halloween pumpkin. Remove seeds and inner stringy flesh. Rinse well.

2. Place hollow pumpkins, with lids on, in a glass casserole pan. Fill pan with ½-inch of water and cover with foil. Bake 45 minutes until pumpkins are tender but not dry. Periodically replenish water to keep pumpkins moist. Set pumpkins aside.

3. Wash chard well and remove thick stems. Place wet chard in a large pot and steam in the water that clings to the leaves for 5 minutes. Drain cooked chard and squeeze out excess moisture. When greens have cooled, chop finely.

4. In a nonstick saucepan, sauté shallots over medium heat until transparent. Add flour and stir with a wire whisk, allowing flour to toast lightly. Slowly add hot water and whisk vigorously to smooth out lumps. Bring to a boil, then lower heat and add seasonings. Continue to simmer 3 to 4 minutes until sauce thickens. Stir in cooked chard and simmer another 5 minutes.

5. Before serving, reheat pumpkins and place on a serving dish. Fill each with several spoonfuls of creamed chard and replace lids.

Calories per serving:	79
Grams of fat:	.8
Percentage fat calories:	9%
Cholesterol:	0 mg.

White Mountain Stuffed Onions

Serves 6

Prep Time: 15 minutes
Cooking Time: 20 minutes

6   medium onions, peeled and halved, with some of the center scooped out

2   tablespoons teriyaki sauce

½   teaspoon mustard

1   tablespoon finely minced onion (from the scooped-out centers of the onions)

1   tablespoon kuzu dissolved in ¼ cup water

1   cup wild rice blend, cooked

½   cup thawed, uncooked frozen peas

1   tablespoon chopped red bell pepper

1   tablespoon gomasio or sesame seeds

For many families, whole onions are a traditional side dish. Here, we've halved and steamed onions (which can be done a day or two ahead of time) and spooned in a bit of mixed grain pilaf enlivened with peas and red pepper morsels. The taste is nicely spiced with mustard — look for natural varieties such as wasabi- or miso-flavored — and natural teriyaki sauce.

1. In a steamer basket, steam onions over moderate heat 20 minutes or until tender but still firm. Transfer to an ovenproof serving dish.

2. Combine teriyaki sauce, 2 tablespoons water and mustard in a small saucepan. Add minced onion and cook over low heat, stirring occasionally, for 5 minutes. Add dissolved kuzu and stir to combine.

3. Combine sauce with rice, peas, pepper and gomasio. Mix thoroughly and spoon into the onions. Cover and keep warm until ready to serve.

Calories per serving:	*149*
Grams of fat:	*1*
Percentage fat calories:	*6%*
Cholesterol:	*0 mg.*

176 ■ SIDE DISHES

DELICIOUS! COLLECTION

Harvest Apple Cups

Serves 6

Prep Time: 15 minutes
Baking Time: 5 to 10 minutes

6   medium all-purpose apples such as Granny Smith

1   medium acorn squash, halved and baked until tender

½   cup applesauce

1   tablespoon maple syrup

1   teaspoon baking blend spice (or ⅓ teaspoon each cinnamon, nutmeg, and allspice)

Apples and squash naturally belong on any early winter feast menu. Here we've filled hollowed apples with a simple squash puree, its sweetness gently enhanced with natural applesauce and a little maple syrup. You can cook the squash ahead of time and refrigerate it until ready to puree and fill the apples.

1. Preheat oven to 350°F. Cut off top quarter of each apple and core, scooping out some of the center to make a cup.

2. Discard seeds from squash (or rinse, bake until crisp and toss with tamari for a healthful snack). Cut squash into cubes and puree in a blender or food processor until smooth.

3. Stir in applesauce, maple syrup and spices. Fill each apple with some of the squash mixture. Bake 5 to 10 minutes until warmed through.

Calories per serving:	121
Grams of fat:	0
Percentage fat calories:	0%
Cholesterol:	0 mg.

Red Pepper Couscous Ring With Vegetables

Serves 8

Prep Time: 40 minutes
Cooking Time: 10 minutes
Chilling Time: 1 hour

3   large red bell peppers, roasted, peeled and seeded

1   garlic clove

½   tablespoon wine vinegar

2   cups whole wheat couscous

3   tablespoons soy margarine

½   medium onion, chopped

    Sea salt and freshly ground black pepper to taste

3   cups lightly steamed vegetables (broccoli, carrots, mushrooms, cauliflower, etc.)

2   cups nonfat plain yogurt

1   tablespoon chopped fresh dill

Whole wheat couscous cooks quickly and has a mild, pleasant flavor. We combined it with roasted red peppers, which gives it a sweet taste and a gorgeous color. The filling may be varied according to the vegetables you have on hand, but the more colorful they are, the more they enhance your table.

1. To roast red peppers, place under broiler or rotate over a gas flame until skin blisters and is completely black on all sides. Place peppers in a paper bag for 15 minutes to cool. Scrape away charred skin, then seed.

2. In a blender or food processor, puree peppers, garlic and vinegar. Scrape into a bowl and set aside.

3. In a large saucepan, bring 4 cups water to a boil. Stir in couscous and margarine, cover and remove from heat. After 10 minutes, stir again to fluff.

3. Add red pepper puree, onion and seasonings to couscous and mix well. Place in a lightly greased ring mold and refrigerate at least an hour.

4. To serve, unmold on a serving plate and fill with vegetables. Combine yogurt and dill in a small bowl and serve as a sauce with the couscous ring.

Calories per serving:	242
Grams of fat:	5.8
Percentage fat calories:	21%
Cholesterol:	0 mg.

Grain & Green Almondine

Serves 4

Prep Time: 5 minutes

2   cups cooked whole grains

1   bunch parsley, stemmed and chopped

½   cup toasted almonds, coarsely chopped

We used a popular natural "breakfast pilaf" of eight whole grains to prepare this simple dish, but any combination of brown rice or other grains will do nicely — even leftovers! Try using quick-cooking brown rice as another option. With potassium from the almonds and vitamin A from the parsley, plus the B vitamins in the grains, this is a very healthful dish. To reduce fat, substitute water chestnuts for the almonds.

1. Combine grains, parsley and almonds and toss to mix well.

Calories per serving:	*211*
Grams of fat:	*10*
Percentage fat calories:	*41%*
Cholesterol:	*0 mg.*

Red Rice With Sun-Dried Tomatoes

Serves 10

Prep Time: 10 minutes
Cooking Time: 20 minutes

1   large onion, chopped

2   garlic cloves, minced

2   tablespoons olive oil

4   cups pasta sauce

6   sun-dried tomatoes,
    coarsely chopped

10 cups cooked brown rice

1   tablespoon chopped fresh
    basil

This rice can be as mildly or assertively spiced as you like. It makes a great accompaniment to chili and is quick to prepare. To save time, the brown rice can be cooked up to a week ahead and frozen in an airtight container. Let it thaw at room temperature, then proceed with the recipe.

1. In a large pot, sauté onion and garlic in olive oil over moderate heat 5 minutes. Stir in pasta sauce, tomatoes, rice and basil, cover and cook 15 minutes or until warmed through.

Calories per serving:	308
Grams of fat:	5.2
Percentage fat calories:	15%
Cholesterol:	0 mg.

North Woods Stuffing Bake

Serves 6

Prep Time: 20 minutes
Cooking Time: 20 minutes

1	tablespoon soy margarine
¼	cup chopped leek or onion
¼	cup chopped celery
1	garlic clove, minced
2	tablespoons arrowroot
½	cup plain soy milk
1	tablespoon mellow miso
2	frozen grain burgers, thawed and crumbled
⅓	cup dried shiitake mushrooms, soaked 20 minutes in warm water and drained, with soaking liquid reserved
1	cup whole-grain stuffing mix
1	cup cooked mixed grain pilaf
1	cup cranberry sauce
1	medium apple, cored and chopped

This hearty casserole complements an organic turkey or chicken. It also makes a robust main dish for guests who prefer strictly vegetarian fare. It's rich with shiitake mushrooms, natural cranberry sauce, mixed grain pilaf and seasonings. We used frozen grain burgers, but you could substitute tofu burger mix or crumbled cooked natural turkey sausage. The creamy (dairy-free!) sauce takes only a few minutes to prepare and makes a flavorful base for this baked delight.

1. To make sauce, melt margarine over moderate heat. Add leek, celery and garlic and sauté until soft, about 5 minutes. Stir in arrowroot and cook, stirring constantly, until liquid is absorbed, about 1 minute. Add enough water to reserved shiitake soaking liquid to make 2 cups. Stir into sautéed vegetables, then whisk in soy milk and miso. (The sauce can be made up to a day ahead and refrigerated until you're ready to finish the casserole.)

2. To assemble the casserole, combine crumbled burgers, mushrooms, stuffing mix, grains, cranberry sauce and apple in a large baking dish. Fold in sauce and bake at 350°F for 20 to 25 minutes. If desired, garnish with fresh cranberries.

Calories per serving:	*340*
Grams of fat:	*1.5*
Percentage fat calories:	*4%*
Cholesterol:	*1 mg.*

Emerald Cress Sauce

Yields 1½ cups

Prep Time: 10 minutes
Cooking Time: 15 minutes

1	tablespoon soy margarine
½	medium onion, chopped
1	cup mashed potatoes
½	cup water
1	pound watercress, stemmed and finely chopped
2	tablespoons lemon juice
	Sea salt and freshly ground black pepper to taste

This is a terrific topping for poached fish or chicken, baked tofu or a simple dish of grains and vegetables. It also makes a great hot or cold soup when thinned with vegetable broth. Check your natural foods store to see if it carries dehydrated potato flakes, which make instant and very tasty mashed potatoes.

1. In a medium saucepan, melt margarine over moderate heat and add onion. Sauté until softened, about 5 minutes.

2. Stir in mashed potatoes and ½ cup water until smooth. Add watercress, lemon juice and seasonings, reduce heat to moderately low, and cook, covered, until watercress is completely softened, 5 to 10 minutes.

Note: *For a subtle variation in taste, substitute spinach, arugula or escarole for watercress.*

Calories per tablespoon:	*14*
Grams of fat:	*.5*
Percentage fat calories:	*31%*
Cholesterol:	*0 mg.*

Miso Mushroom Gravy

Yields 3 cups

Prep Time: 10 minutes
Cooking Time: 25 minutes

1	tablespoon sesame oil
1	pound mushrooms, sliced
1	onion, sliced
1	tablespoon arrowroot
2	tablespoons mellow miso
1½	cups water
1	tablespoon Worcestershire sauce
	Sea salt and freshly ground black pepper, to taste

Rich and savory, this versatile gravy tastes great over nut loaf, vegetable or grain burgers, tofu or even plain brown rice. If desired, you can substitute kuzu (also known as "wild arrowroot") for the arrowroot.

1. In a large saucepan, cook mushrooms and onions in sesame oil over moderately low heat for 10 minutes until the mushrooms release their juices.

2. Dissolve miso, arrowroot and Worcestershire sauce in ¼ cup water and stir into mushroom mixture. Add remaining water, increase heat to moderate and cook 15 minutes, stirring occasionally until thickened. Season with salt and pepper as desired.

Calories per tablespoon:	9.4
Grams of fat:	.4
Percentage fat calories:	36%
Cholesterol:	0 mg.

Cucumber Dill Dressing

<u>Yields 1 cup</u>

Prep Time: 10 minutes

1   large cucumber, seeded peeled and cut into large chunks

2   shallots, chopped

1   garlic clove, minced

1   tablespoon fresh lemon juice

2   tablespoons white wine vinegar

2   tablespoons honey

1   tablespoon tahini

3   tablespoons chopped fresh dill or 1 tablespoon dried dill

¾   cup plain soy milk

It takes just minutes to buzz up this tangy dressing, a perfect complement to cold steamed artichokes, cold vegetable salads or poached fish. You can puree it to as smooth a texture as you like, although we prefer it with small chunks of cucumber and wisps of fresh dill.

1. Place cucumber, shallots, garlic, lemon juice, vinegar, honey and tahini in a blender or food processor. Process briefly, then add dill and soy milk. Puree until only small chunks of cucumber are visible.

Calories per tablespoon:	22
Grams of fat:	.7
Percentage fat calories:	30%
Cholesterol:	0 mg.

Onion Mint Raita

Yields 2 cups

Prep Time: 10 minutes
Cooking Time: 1 minute

2   medium red onions, thinly sliced

2   cups nonfat plain yogurt

⅓ cup chopped fresh mint

Sea salt and freshly ground black pepper to taste

2   finely minced hot green chilies

Here's an intriguing, Indian-inspired condiment, which makes a pleasant salad or cooling accompaniment to fiery curries. To avoid the discomfort some people experience with raw onions, these are briefly immersed in boiling water, which makes them much more digestible and succulent.

1. In a medium saucepan, bring 1 quart water to a boil. Remove from heat, add onions and drain after 30 seconds. Rinse onions in cold water and drain well.

2. In a medium bowl, combine yogurt, mint, salt, pepper and chilies. Stir in onions and mix well.

Calories per tablespoon:	15
Grams of fat:	.02
Percentage fat calories:	1%
Cholesterol:	0 mg.

Corn Raisin Relish

Yields 2 cups

Prep Time: 10 minutes
Cooking Time: 15 minutes

2   cups corn kernels

1   cup seedless raisins

½   cup apple cider vinegar

¼   teaspoon chili powder

2   tablespoons granulated cane juice or brown rice syrup

1   tablespoon chopped fresh parsley

2   tablespoons chopped pimiento or red bell pepper

This tangy, sweet-and-sour relish brightens every bite of tofu, chicken or turkey hot dogs. It also jazzes up a cheese sandwich in the nicest way. Store in a jar in the refrigerator for up to a week — if it lasts that long!

1. In a medium saucepan, combine corn, raisins, vinegar, chili powder and sweetener. Bring to a boil.

2. Reduce heat to moderately low and simmer until liquid is absorbed, about 5 minutes. Mix in chopped parsley and pimiento and let cool.

Calories per tablespoon:	16
Grams of fat:	.1
Percentage fat calories:	5%
Cholesterol:	0 mg.

Winter Apple Chutney

<u>Yields 2 cups</u>

Prep Time: 10 minutes
Cooking Time: 10 to 20
    minutes

1	cup dried apples, coarsely chopped
1	cup applesauce
⅓	cup brown rice vinegar
⅓	cup granulated cane juice or maple granules
1	small onion, chopped
¼	cup seedless raisins
1	tablespoon fresh ginger, minced
1	large garlic clove, minced
½	teaspoon hot sauce, or to taste

Blend the sweetness of apples with the spiciness of onion and hot sauce for a truly original chutney that adds zip to grain dishes like couscous or millet.

1. In a saucepan, combine all ingredients and bring to a boil over moderately high heat, stirring occasionally for 15 minutes. If microwaving, combine all ingredients in a glass bowl. Microwave uncovered on high until slightly thickened and bubbling, about 8 minutes.

2. Let cool slightly. Puree ½ cup of the mixture in a blender or food processor and then mix with remaining chutney. Serve at room temperature or chilled.

Calories per tablespoon:	20
Grams of fat:	0
Percentage fat calories:	0%
Cholesterol:	0 mg.

Crimson Cranberry Glaze

Yields 4 cups

Prep Time: 5 minutes
Cooking Time: 10 minutes

2   cups cranberry nectar
frozen concentrate (for a
less intense sauce, use
cranberry juice instead of
the frozen concentrate)

2   cups currant jelly or
cranberry jelly

Serve this tangy glaze as a relish sauce to enhance Royal Tofu Roulade and Wild Rice Stuffing (page 144) or to perk up any special meal.

1.   Mix ingredients in a blender until smooth.

2.   In a small saucepan, bring cranberry sauce to a boil, lower heat and simmer for 5 minutes until sauce becomes a thick glaze.

Calories per tablespoon:	37
Grams of fat:	0
Percentage fat calories:	0%
Cholesterol:	0 mg.

How Sweet It Is!

How Sweet It Is!

If you can't imagine a birthday party without cake and ice cream, holidays without pies and cookies or Valentine's Day without chocolates, you're not alone. Americans are hooked on sweets. We all indulge occasionally . . . and feel guilty afterward.

However, desserts can be a nutritious, low-fat, guiltless part of your diet when made with unrefined whole-meal flours, fresh or dried fruits, unprocessed oils and natural flavorings and sweeteners like molasses, honey and concentrated fruit juice.

With the *Delicious!* dessert ideas we've assembled here, you can have your cake and eat it too. We've substituted tofu for cream cheese in our Yin-Yang Tofu Cheesecake (page 205) to reduce fat and eliminate cholesterol without sacrificing richness. And our fresh fruit desserts like Fresh Fruit With Island Citrus Sauce (page 192) are virtually fat-free goodies that will satisfy any sweet tooth.

Here are some of our favorite Delicious! *suggestions for skimming fat and reducing sugar in desserts:*

- When baking cakes and cookies, substitute 2 egg whites for each whole egg or use egg replacer (see our formula for egg replacer on page 35). Replace white sugar with natural sweeteners like honey, maple syrup, molasses, granulated cane juice, barley malt or rice syrup. Consult our "Sweet Talk" chart on the following page for how to substitute natural sweeteners for white sugar in baked goods.

- Thicken puddings and mousses with agar (a flavorless sea vegetable) instead of gelatin (an animal product).

- In place of cream cheese in pies and cheesecakes, use kefir cream cheese, yogurt cheese, silken tofu or amazake.

- Substitute carob for chocolate in cakes, cookies, mousses and dessert sauces. Carob, which is produced by grinding and roasting locust tree pods, has the appearance of chocolate but none of the caffeine and one-tenth the fat. And it's available in several forms: powder, chips and syrup.

- For an alternative to whipped cream that's cholesterol free, whip silken tofu in a blender with maple syrup.

Sweet Talk:
How To Convert Recipes

Reaching for the maple syrup instead of sugar? Use this chart to determine how much of a particular natural sweetener to substitute for white sugar and whether the proportion of liquid ingredients should change.

SWEETENER	SUBSTITUTION FOR 1 CUP SUGAR	REDUCTION OF TOTAL LIQUID
Barley Malt & Rice Syrup	1½ cups	slightly
Concentrated Fruit Juice Sweetener	1½ cups	⅛ cup
Date Sugar	⅔ cup	—
Honey	¾ cup	⅛ cup
Granulated Cane Juice	½ cup	—
Maple Granules	1 cup	—
Maple Syrup	¾ cup	⅛ cup
Molasses	½ cup	—

Fresh Fruit With Island Citrus Sauce

Serves 4

Prep Time: 5 minutes
Cooking Time: 5 to 10 minutes

½   **cup lemonade**

½   **cup orange marmalade**

1   **kiwi fruit, peeled and sliced**

1   **orange, peeled and sliced**

½   **pint strawberries, washed and hulled**

Colorful kiwi fruit, orange slices and strawberries are combined in a sumptuous sweet-tart sauce to create this very low-fat dessert.

1. In a small saucepan, mix lemonade and marmalade. Bring to a boil, then reduce heat and simmer 5 minutes, stirring occasionally until thickened.

2. To serve, spoon equal portions of sauce onto 4 plates. Arrange fruit on top of sauce and garnish with orange peel, if desired.

Calories per serving:	144
Grams of fat:	.3
Percentage fat calories:	2%
Cholesterol:	0 mg.

Blueberry Apple Juice Crown

Serves 6 to 8

Prep Time: 10 minutes
Cooking Time: 15 minutes
Chilling Time: 2 hours

2   quarts apple-raspberry or
    apple juice

1   cup agar flakes

    **Dash of vanilla extract
    and nutmeg**

2   cups fresh blueberries

    **Sliced kiwi, peaches,
    nectarines and cashews
    for garnish**

A natural substitute for gelatin, agar is sold in a variety of forms including bars and flakes. Check the package for directions on the proper amount of agar to use for molding since it may vary with the product's form.

1. In a large saucepan, bring juice, agar, vanilla and nutmeg to a boil. Stir occasionally until agar is completely dissolved, about 10 minutes. Reduce heat to a simmer, add berries and cook 5 minutes longer.

2. Lightly oil a 2-quart mold (a ring mold is nice, but a leakproof springform pan or even a shallow bowl will work). Pour in juice mixture and refrigerate until chilled. To serve, unmold and garnish with fresh seasonal fruit and nuts.

Calories per serving:	*123*
Grams of fat:	*0*
Percentage fat calories:	*0%*
Cholesterol:	*0 mg.*

Caribbean Banana Bake

Serves 4

Prep Time: 10 minutes
Cooking Time: 8 minutes

4	firm ripe bananas
2	tablespoons lime juice
½	cup orange marmalade
1	teaspoon allspice
¼	cup water
¼	cup currants or raisins
¼	cup diced dried papaya
2	tablespoons chopped peanuts

Bubbling hot bananas are smothered with an assortment of dried fruit and nuts in this Caribbean-style treat.

1. Preheat broiler to high. Peel bananas, slice and toss with lime juice. Place in a shallow baking dish and set aside.

2. In a skillet, combine marmalade, allspice, water, currants and papaya. Simmer 5 minutes. Pour mixture over bananas and broil, tossing occasionally, until bananas are hot. Transfer to serving bowls. Top with peanuts.

Calories per serving:	270
Grams of fat:	3
Percentage fat calories:	10%
Cholesterol:	0 mg.

Carob Fondue With Strawberries

Yields 2 cups sauce

Prep Time: 5 minutes
Cooking Time: 15 minutes

3	tablespoons soy margarine
10	ounces unsweetened carob chips
½	teaspoon grated nutmeg
1	teaspoon vanilla extract
½	cup maple syrup
¾	cup nonfat dairy milk or 1% fat soy milk
2	pints fresh strawberries, washed

Now that plump fresh strawberries are available year round, you can celebrate special occasions with a treat that everyone will love. This velvety fondue plays up the strawberries' juicy sweetness.

1. In a fondue pot over a low flame or the top of a double boiler set over hot water, combine margarine, carob chips, nutmeg, vanilla, maple syrup and milk. Stir until carob chips are melted, about 15 minutes. Serve with fresh strawberries for dipping.

Calories per tablespoon:	68
Grams of fat:	3.3
Percentage fat calories:	44%
Cholesterol:	0 mg.

Basic Wholesome Crepes

Yields 12 crepes

Prep Time: 5 minutes
Chilling Time: 1 hour
Cooking Time: 20 minutes

½   cup whole wheat pastry flour

¾   cup nonfat dairy milk or 1% fat soy milk

1   egg

2   egg whites

1½ tablespoons soy margarine, melted and cooled

Crepes transform fresh fruit into a satisfying dessert. With our low-fat recipe, you can make spectacular desserts to showcase any fresh seasonal fruit. The recipe below makes about 12 crepes. The extras freeze well and are great to have on hand for quick desserts, breakfasts and entrees. Substitute a natural pancake mix, if desired, but be prepared for a final product that is slightly more puffy.

1. In a food processor or blender, combine flour, milk, egg, egg whites and soy margarine and process until smooth. (Or beat with a rotary beater until blended.) If possible, chill batter at least an hour before preparing crepes.

2. Brush an 8-inch skillet or crepe pan with vegetable oil and heat until water dances on the surface. Pour in about 2 tablespoons of batter, lifting and tilting the pan so that it is completely covered by batter. Cook each crepe on one side only, about 2 minutes, or until edges begin to brown. Turn out, cooked side up, on a plate or clean kitchen towel. Repeat with remaining batter.

Calories per serving:	*57*
Grams of fat:	*2*
Percentage fat calories:	*31%*
Cholesterol:	*0 mg.*

Crepe Blossoms With Berry Sauce

Serves 4

Prep Time: 10 minutes
Cooking Time: 8 minutes

4   **Basic Wholesome Crepes
      (page 196)**

2   **cups lemon sorbet**

½   **cup raspberry syrup**

1   **cup red raspberries**

Here's a stunning recipe that's deceptively low-fat.

1. Preheat oven to 400°F. Fit each crepe into ovenproof custard cups or muffin tins. Place a ball of aluminum foil in the middle of each crepe to keep it open. Bake 5 minutes. Remove foil balls and bake 2 or 3 minutes longer until golden brown. Cool and carefully remove.

2. To serve, spoon 2 tablespoons syrup onto each serving plate. Place a crepe blossom on each dish and fill with ½ cup sorbet. Top each with ¼ cup raspberries and enjoy immediately.

Calories per serving:	*247*
Grams of fat:	*3.4*
Percentage fat calories:	*12%*
Cholesterol:	*0 mg.*

Strawberry Yogurt Whip

Serves 4

Prep Time: 5 minutes

1   cup nonfat plain yogurt

2   tablespoons honey

1   cup sliced fresh strawberries plus 4 whole berries for garnish

2   tablespoons raw wheat germ

1   cup crushed ice

½   cup sparkling water

    Fresh mint sprigs for garnish

Other low-calorie fresh fruits such as blueberries may be substituted for strawberries in this delicate frappé.

1. In a blender or food processor, blend yogurt, honey, strawberries, wheat germ, ice and sparkling water until frothy.

2. Pour into parfait glasses and garnish with fresh berries and mint sprigs. Serve immediately.

Calories per serving:	*84*
Grams of fat:	*.5*
Percentage fat calories:	*5%*
Cholesterol:	*0 mg.*

Snowy Lemon Mousse

Serves 2

Prep Time: 15 minutes
Cooking Time: 10 minutes
Chilling Time: 1 hour

1   lemon, thinly sliced

2   cups lemonade

1   cake soft tofu (about ½ pound)

   Lemon twists for garnish

Fresh lemon has a refreshing flavor, and this dairy-free mousse will satisfy any dessert cravings. Serve it in hollowed lemon shells for an attractive presentation.

1.   In a medium saucepan, combine lemon with enough lemonade to cover. Bring to a boil, then reduce heat to moderately low. Cover and simmer 10 minutes until soft.

2.   Let cool slightly, then transfer to a blender or food processor and chop coarsely. Gradually add tofu (in batches if necessary) and puree until uniformly combined. There should be chunks of lemon remaining.

3.   Pour into serving dishes and chill 1 hour until set. Garnish with lemon twists.

Calories per serving:	*179*
Grams of fat:	*3.8*
Percentage fat calories:	*19%*
Cholesterol:	*0 mg.*

Raspberry Passion Mousse

Serves 8

Prep Time: 10 minutes
Chilling Time: 1 hour

1   tablespoon agar flakes

¼   cup raspberry cider

½   pound silken tofu

3   tablespoons honey

3   cups sliced, frozen, un-
      sweetened raspberries,
      thawed and drained

1   teaspoon vanilla

If you have a passion for raspberries, this is for you! With frozen organic fruit available, you can serve this rich-tasting dessert year round. And mousses don't need heavy cream to be ambrosial! Agar does a terrific job of helping molds and puddings keep their shape, even at room temperature. Tofu adds rich creaminess.

1. Dissolve agar in cider. In a blender or food processor, combine all ingredients, adding raspberries a cup at a time. Blend on low, allowing some berries to remain in chunks.

2. Pour into parfait glasses and chill 1 hour until set. If desired, garnish with a dollop of sweetened nonfat yogurt and fresh raspberries.

Calories per serving:	75
Grams of fat:	1.5
Percentage fat calories:	18%
Cholesterol:	0 mg.

Carob Swirl Mousse

Serves 4

Prep Time: 15 minutes
Chilling Time: 1 hour

1 cup sweetened carob chips

⅓ cup maple syrup

10 ounces silken tofu

½ cup nonfat plain yogurt

Serve this decadent mousse with fresh or frozen organic raspberries.

1. Combine carob with maple syrup in the top of a double boiler and place over simmering water. Stir occasionally until chips are melted.

2. Drain tofu. In a food processor, puree tofu and yogurt until smooth. With motor running, add ¾ of the melted carob mixture to the tofu. Continue to process until thoroughly blended.

3. Spoon mousse into serving dishes. Pour reserved carob mixture on top and cut into mousse a few times to create a swirled effect. Cover and chill at least 1 hour. This recipe may be prepared two days in advance.

Calories per serving:	*321*
Grams of fat:	*12.3*
Percentage fat calories:	*34%*
Cholesterol:	*0 mg.*

Vanilla Berry Trifle

Serves 16

Prep Time: 20 minutes
Cooking Time: 35 minutes

2   packages whole-grain
    cake mix

1   10-ounce jar strawberry
    preserves

1   cup toasted slivered
    almonds

2   pints fresh strawberries,
    washed and hulled

2½ cups vanilla low-fat
    yogurt

This dazzling dessert will elicit exclamations of pleasure from your guests, yet it's so simple to assemble that you don't need a special occasion to enjoy it. The recipe is a healthy adaptation of a classic Victorian dessert made with lady fingers, liqueurs and a rich egg custard. They're replaced with whole-grain cake, jam and vanilla yogurt.

1. Prepare cake mixes as directed and bake in 9-inch round cake pans. Turn out onto a rack to cool, then spread with some of the preserves and cut into 1-inch pieces.

2. Line the bottom of a deep glass bowl with some of the cake pieces and sprinkle with some of the almonds. Slice 1 pint of the strawberries and make a layer on top of the cake.

3. Continue layering cake, preserves, almonds and berries, ending with a layer of cake. Pour yogurt over trifle and garnish decoratively with whole strawberries.

Calories per serving:	312
Grams of fat:	9.5
Percentage fat calories:	28%
Cholesterol:	26.5 mg.

Lemon Berry Gingersnap Pie

Serves 8

Prep Time: 15 minutes
Cooking Time: 10 minutes
Chilling Time: 1 hour

2   cups crumbled gingersnap
     cookies (one 8-ounce
     package)

4   tablespoons (½ stick)
     soy margarine, melted

½   teaspoon ground ginger

3   cups lemon sorbet,
     softened, (1½ pints)

¾   cup blueberry preserves

12   gingersnaps for garnish

     Fresh blueberries for
     garnish, if desired

This dramatic-looking frozen pie sparkles with the refreshing complementary flavors of lemon and ginger. As an added plus, lemon sorbet is naturally low in calories.

1. Preheat oven to 350°F. Combine gingersnap crumbs, melted margarine and ginger and press into a 9-inch pie plate. Bake 10 to 12 minutes until crust is set.

2. Swirl blueberry preserves into softened sorbet. (If desired, you can also mix in some fresh berries.) Spoon into pie crust and arrange whole gingersnaps around the edge. Garnish with fresh blueberries. Return pie to the freezer for at least an hour. Twenty minutes before serving, transfer pie to refrigerator.

Calories per serving:	*342*
Grams of fat:	*13*
Percentage fat calories:	*34%*
Cholesterol:	*0 mg.*

Amazing Raspberry-Banana Flan

Serves 6

Prep Time: 15 minutes
Baking Time: 30 minutes

1½ cups cookie crumbs

2   tablespoons melted soy
    margarine

6   bananas, peeled and cut
    into chunks

1   cup nonfat plain yogurt

2   tablespoons raspberry
    preserves

Fresh raspberries and
mint leaves for garnish

*The filling of this easy-to-make pie becomes custardy
when baked. Vary the flavor with fresh blueberries and
blueberry preserves or any other favorite fruit.*

1. Preheat oven to 400°F. Combine cookie crumbs and
    melted margarine and press into the bottom and sides
    of an 8-inch pie or tart pan.

2. With a potato masher, mash bananas and beat in
    half the yogurt and 1 tablespoon preserves. Pour into
    pie crust and spoon in remaining yogurt and
    preserves, smoothing the top. Bake 25 to 30 minutes
    until top is almost firm (it will set as it cools).
    Garnish with raspberries and mint.

Calories per serving:	309
Grams of fat:	7.7
Percentage fat calories:	22%
Cholesterol:	0 mg.

Yin-Yang Tofu Cheesecake

Serves 12

Prep Time: 20 minutes
Baking Time: 30 minutes

15   small oat bran or amaranth graham crackers

3   tablespoons soy margarine, melted

½   teaspoon cinnamon

5   cakes soft tofu (about 3½ pounds), coarsely crumbled

⅔   cup plain or vanilla 1% fat soy milk

¼   cup tahini

¾   cup maple syrup

2   egg whites

2   tablespoons lemon juice

1½ teaspoons vanilla extract

Fresh fruit such as grapes, blueberries, apricots or peaches

This dreamy cake keeps well in the refrigerator for several days, and the recipe can easily be halved for smaller households. You won't believe how creamy and dense it is!

1. In a blender or food processor, grind graham crackers into coarse crumbs (or place them in a plastic bag, wrap in a dish towel and crumble with a rolling pin). Pour into an 8- or 9-inch springform pan and add margarine and cinnamon. Stir well to combine and press firmly on the bottom of the pan.

2. Preheat oven to 350°F. In a blender or food processor, puree tofu in batches until smooth, adding about a tablespoon of soy milk with each batch. Scrape into a large bowl. Stir in tahini, maple syrup, egg whites, vanilla extract and lemon juice and mix well.

3. Scrape into the prepared pan and smooth the top with a spatula. Bake 30 minutes until filling is set and top begins to turn golden. Cool on a rack, then cover and refrigerate until chilled.

4. Arrange fruit on top in a yin-yang pattern or in any fashion that pleases you.

Calories per serving:	214
Grams of fat:	12.8
Percentage fat calories:	54%
Cholesterol:	0 mg.

Valentine Berry Cake

Serves 12

Prep Time: 10 minutes
Baking Time: 30 minutes

1 package whole-grain cake mix

1 cup skim milk ricotta cheese

1 teaspoon honey

1 teaspoon vanilla extract

1 pint strawberries or raspberries

Believe it or not, this is a cake that weight watchers can enjoy, with only 192 calories per slice. Elegant and simple, it's a great shortcut dessert for a special dinner. The creamy white frosting only looks rich — it's actually whipped ricotta cheese, lightly sweetened.

1. Preheat oven to 350°F and prepare cake mix according to package directions. Scrape batter into a greased 8-inch heart-shaped pan (or a square 8-inch cake pan) and bake as directed.

2. To make frosting, place ricotta cheese in a blender or food processor and process about 1 minute until smooth. Beat in honey and vanilla and refrigerate until ready to use.

3. Remove cake from oven and place on a wire rack to cool. When completely cool, make a border of frosting around the cake and decorate with berries. Slice and serve with additional topping and berries, if you wish.

Variations: *Substitute frozen fruit or seedless grapes for fresh berries.*

Calories per serving:	192
Grams of fat:	4
Percentage fat calories:	19%
Cholesterol:	21 mg.

Banana-Lemon Carrot Cake

Serves 8

Prep Time: 30 minutes
Cooking Time: 30 to 35 minutes

1   ripe banana, mashed

1   egg

½   cup maple syrup

¼   cup melted soy margarine, cooled

2   tablespoons nonfat plain yogurt

½   cup water

     Juice and grated rind of ½ lemon

½   teaspoon cinnamon

1   package carrot cake mix

Ricotta-Honey Icing:

¼   cup minus 1 teaspoon honey

1   cup skim milk ricotta cheese

1   cup cream cheese

1   tablespoon nonfat dairy milk or 1% fat soy milk

½   teaspoon vanilla extract

This moist and slightly tropical-flavored cake tastes so good when it's warm from the oven that it doesn't need any frosting. For a splurge, however, you might like it with a liberal coating of Ricotta-Honey Icing.

1. Preheat oven to 350°F. In a large bowl, combine banana, egg, syrup, margarine, yogurt, water, lemon juice and rind. Beat until creamy. Fold in cinnamon and cake mix until well-combined.

2. Scrape batter into a well-greased 8-inch square cake pan. Bake 30 to 35 minutes until a toothpick inserted in the center comes out clean. Wait 10 minutes, then turn out onto a rack to cool. If desired, frost with Ricotta-Honey Icing.

3. To make icing, combine honey, ricotta cheese, cream cheese, milk and vanilla in a blender or food processor and blend until smooth.

Calories per serving:	*393*
Grams of fat:	*16.7*
Percentage fat calories:	*38%*
Cholesterol:	*59 mg.*

Molasses Gingerbread With Lemon Sauce

Serves 9

Prep Time: 25 minutes
Cooking Time: 25 to 30 minutes

¼	cup honey
½	cup vegetable oil
1	egg
3	egg whites
1	cup molasses
1	cup buttermilk
1	14-ounce package bran muffin mix
½	teaspoon cinnamon
½	teaspoon ground ginger
½	teaspoon ground nutmeg

Sauce:

1	tablespoon arrowroot
1½	cups plain soy milk
1	cinnamon stick
	Grated rind of 2 lemons
¼	cup fresh lemon juice
¼	cup honey

Dark, fragrant gingerbread has to be one of the coziest foods around. Served with fresh Lemon Sauce, it's wonderful for dessert, brunch, tea or coffee breaks and just plain snacking! Natural bran muffin mix speeds up the preparation and supplies dietary fiber.

1. Preheat oven to 350°F. In a large bowl, beat honey with oil. Add egg and egg whites one at a time, beating well after each addition. Beat in molasses.

2. Stir in buttermilk, bran muffin mix, cinnamon, ginger and nutmeg. Pour into a greased 8-inch square baking dish and bake 25 to 30 minutes until top is just firm. Serve with Lemon Sauce.

3. To make sauce, dissolve arrowroot in 2 tablespoons soy milk in a medium saucepan off the heat. Add remaining milk and cinnamon stick and place over moderately low heat. Stir until thick enough to coat spoon.

4. Stir in lemon rind, juice and honey. Remove cinnamon stick and drizzle sauce over gingerbread. Any remaining sauce can be refrigerated and reheated slowly in a double boiler over warm water.

Calories per serving:	468
Grams of fat:	15.8
Percentage fat calories:	30%
Cholesterol:	25 mg.

Autumn Apple Crisp

Serves 8

Prep Time: 15 minutes
Cooking Time: 30 minutes

5   apples, cored and sliced
    (about 4 cups)

1   cup apple juice

2   cups whole-grain cereal
    or granola

1½ teaspoons baking blend
    spice (or ½ teaspoon
    each cinnamon, nutmeg
    and allspice)

6   tablespoons soy
    margarine

¾   cup whole wheat pastry
    flour

Warm apple crisp topped with a scoop of vanilla ice cream (try soy or rice ice cream products for a healthful change) is a sublime treat. Pears would work equally well in this dish.

1. Preheat oven to 350°F. Place apples in a rectangular baking dish and pour on apple juice.

2. In a shallow bowl, use a pastry blender or two forks to combine cereal, spices, margarine and flour until mixture resembles coarse meal. Sprinkle over apples and bake 30 minutes until apples are soft.

Calories per serving:	*300*
Grams of fat:	*13.6*
Percentage fat calories:	*41%*
Cholesterol:	*0 mg.*

Carob & Cream Hearts

Yields 1 dozen sandwich cookies

Prep Time: 7 minutes
Cooking Time: 10 to 12 minutes

1   cup soy margarine, softened

½   cup honey

1   egg

¾   cup carob powder

4   cups whole wheat pastry flour

¼   teaspoon baking powder

½   teaspoon sea salt (optional)

1   teaspoon vanilla (optional)

4   ounces cream cheese

4   tablespoons strawberry preserves

These light cookies have a delicate carob flavor. They're delicious on their own, but for a special occasion you may wish to sandwich them with a strawberry cream cheese filling. To keep the edges of cut-out cookies crisp and defined, bake them on chilled cookie sheets. Take care to check the cookies while they're baking, as carob has a tendency to overbrown.

1. In a large mixing bowl, cream margarine with honey and egg. Gradually add carob powder, flour and baking powder. Mix dough well until it has the consistency of soft modeling clay.

2. Preheat oven to 350°F. On a floured surface, roll out dough about ¼-inch thick and cut into shapes with cookie cutter.

3. Bake on a greased cookie sheet until crisp, about 10 to 12 minutes. Remove from cookie sheet to cool.

4. While cookies are cooling, blend cream cheese and strawberry preserves in a food processor or by hand. To serve, sandwich cookies with cream cheese filling.

Calories per serving:	*392*
Grams of fat:	*18.8*
Percentage fat calories:	*43%*
Cholesterol:	*41 mg.*

Amaranth Shortbread

Yields 1 to 1½ dozen

Prep Time: 15 minutes
Cooking Time: 20 minutes

- 2 tablespoons amaranth seed
- ¾ cup whole wheat pastry flour
- ¾ cup rice baking mix
- ¼ cup (½ stick) soy margarine, cut into pieces
- ¼ cup mayonnaise
- ⅓ cup maple syrup

The nutty-flavored grain known as amaranth was favored by the ancient Aztecs and is presently being hailed as a valuable modern food. It contains high quality protein and is especially rich in lysine, an amino acid that's often lacking in other grains. In this recipe, amaranth adds a pleasing crunch reminiscent of cornmeal, while soy margarine and — surprise! — mayonnaise give the shortbreads chewiness. Chilling the dough makes it easier to roll.

1. Preheat oven to 350°F. In a mixing bowl, stir together amaranth, flour and baking mix.

2. Using two knives or a pastry blender, cut in margarine and mayonnaise until mixture is uniformly crumbly. Stir in maple syrup and knead briefly until dough is smooth.

3. Place on a lightly floured surface and roll out to ½-inch thickness. Using a cookie cutter, cut into shapes and transfer to a lightly greased baking sheet.

4. Bake 20 minutes until edges are just beginning to brown. Transfer with a pancake turner to a rack to cool.

Calories per serving:	*170*
Grams of fat:	*8.2*
Percentage fat calories:	*43%*
Cholesterol:	*0 mg.*

Hot Cross Buns With Milk & Honey Glaze

Yields 1 dozen buns

Prep Time: 20 minutes
Cooking Time: 30 minutes

	Whole-grain biscuit mix for 12 muffins
½	cup maple sugar
¼	cup nonfat dry milk powder
1	tablespoon barley malt syrup or rice syrup
1	tablespoon unsalted soy margarine
¼	cup honey

Hot cross buns are the quintessential Easter bread. This is a fast and easy way to make them.

1. Preheat oven to 350°F. Prepare biscuit mix according to package directions. Bake as directed, then turn out onto a rack to cool.

2. Meanwhile, in a small, heavy saucepan combine maple sugar, milk powder, malt syrup and margarine and bring to a boil over moderate heat, stirring until sugar is dissolved. Boil 1 minute, then stir in honey and boil 3 minutes longer.

3. Remove from heat and stir constantly with a wooden spoon until glaze is thickened slightly. Use a tablespoon to pour glaze on top of buns in a cross shape.

Calories per serving:	229
Grams of fat:	5.5
Percentage fat calories:	22%
Cholesterol:	<1 mg.

Light & Fluffy Cheesecake Bites

Yields 24 cakes

Draining Time: 30 minutes
Prep Time: 10 minutes
Cooking Time: 35 minutes

12 ounces low-fat cottage
    cheese, drained

1   tablespoon rice bran

1   whole egg

2   egg whites

¼   cup frozen apple juice
    concentrate, undiluted

¼   cup frozen pineapple
    juice concentrate,
    undiluted

½   teaspoon vanilla extract

1   teaspoon almond extract

⅓   cup nonfat plain yogurt

3   tablespoons maple syrup

These low-fat cheesecake bites are laced with the scent of almond.

1. Place cottage cheese in a strainer over the sink and drain for 30 minutes. Preheat oven to 300°F. Line miniature muffin tins with paper liners.

2. Combine cheese with rice bran in a food processor fitted with chopping blade and process until smooth. Add whole egg, egg whites, juice concentrates and extracts and process to combine.

3. Fill muffin tins ⅔ full with batter. Bake 35 minutes or until a tester comes out clean. Cool on rack, then refrigerate.

4. Combine yogurt with maple syrup. Top each cake with yogurt mixture.

Calories per piece:	*34*
Grams of fat:	*.4*
Percentage fat calories:	*10%*
Cholesterol:	*9.5 mg.*

Carob Peanut Butter Kisses

Yields about 50 pieces

Prep Time: 20 minutes
Chilling Time: 30 minutes

12   ounces unsweetened
     carob chips

½   cup nonfat dairy milk or
     1% fat soy milk

1   tablespoon unsalted soy
     margarine, softened

1   cup maple syrup or maple
     granules

2   cups peanut butter

This recipe offers a rich-tasting alternative to typically oversweetened fudge. Carob, unlike chocolate, is naturally sweet and doesn't require refined sugar to taste good. It is also a source of vitamin A and the B vitamins. Be sure to store these confections in the refrigerator.

1. Melt carob chips, milk and margarine in the top of a double boiler set over hot (not boiling) water.

2. In a medium bowl, combine maple syrup and peanut butter.

3. Cover a jelly roll pan or baking sheet with waxed paper. Spread peanut butter mixture over the pan, patting it evenly with your fingers. Freeze until firm, about 10 minutes.

4. Remove from the freezer and cover with melted carob mixture. Cut into bite-size squares. Freeze 20 minutes before serving.

Variations: *Add ½ cup coarsely chopped dates or raisins. For smoother, richer kisses, add ½ cup softened, unsalted soy margarine in Step 2. Substitute mint carob chips for regular.*

Calories per piece:	120
Grams of fat:	7
Percentage fat calories:	53%
Cholesterol:	0 mg.

Shake It Up!

Shake It Up!

If you've ever whipped up a power-packed smoothie for breakfast or a sumptuous shake for dessert, you already know the simple pleasures of blenderized drinks. When you're on the go, a breakfast shake can be a nourishing meal. Just toss a few healthy ingredients in a blender and whirl up a wholesome, filling drink.

Why not start your day with our quick and healthy Protein Punch Shake (page 217) made with pineapple juice and nutritional yeast? For a satisfying, end-of-the day treat, enjoy a *Delicious!* Carob Malted Soy Shake (page 220).

Here are some shake basics to help you create your own luscious smoothies:
- Use a fruit juice base such as apple, papaya, strawberry or cranberry. Or try flavored soy milk.
- For a heartier shake, add plain or fruit-flavored yogurt or silken tofu.
- For a thick and creamy shake, add a frozen banana and your favorite fruit such as strawberries, blueberries, peaches or mangoes.
- For a slushy shake, add ice cubes.
- To power up a breakfast shake, add one of these energy boosters: protein powder, wheat germ, nutritional yeast, natural malt powder, bee pollen, spirulina or sunflower seeds.

In addition to shakes, we've incorporated recipes for simple summertime thirst quenchers and winter warm-ups. On a long, hot summer day, rejuvenate with Herbed Lemon Melonade (page 227), an effervescent fruit juice and sparkling water concoction, or Cherry Chocolate Fizz (page 229), a frothy soy spritzer reminiscent of oldtime fountain sodas. When winter has you chilled to the bone, sip a soothing fruit juice toddy like Hot Apple Flash (page 230) to bring back that healthy glow.

Cheers!

Protein Punch Shake

Serves 1

Prep Time: 5 minutes

- ¾   cup pineapple or piña colada juice
- ¼   cup plain or vanilla 1% fat soy milk
- 1   frozen banana
- 1   tablespoon nutritional yeast
- ½   teaspoon bee pollen

Frozen bananas add texture and potassium to this shake. To freeze bananas, peel, rub a bit of lemon juice on them and wrap in airtight plastic. Not only does a frozen banana cool down any shake, it's a satisfying, low-cal snack on a hot day. You may or may not want to add nutritional yeast and bee pollen for an extra boost.

1. Combine all ingredients in a blender and puree until smooth.

Calories per serving:	*422*
Grams of fat:	*2.2*
Percentage fat calories:	*5%*
Cholesterol:	*0 mg.*

Sprinter's Ginseng Smoothie

Serves 2

Prep Time: 5 minutes

1½ cups vanilla 1% fat soy
    milk

⅓   cup soft tofu

1   frozen banana

1   medium nectarine or
    peach, chopped

½   cup strawberries or blue-
    berries

1   tablespoon fruit juice-
    sweetened pancake syrup
    (blueberry or strawberry)

    One vial of liquid ginseng
    (about 3 teaspoons)

Oriental ginseng, the revered root the Chinese have used for thousands of years as a tonic, stimulant and body strengthener, gives this power drink an extra boost. (Although vitamin C has been said to neutralize ginseng's effects, there is no evidence to prove this. Ginseng taken as part of this shake, however, may not have the same boost as it would if taken alone.) Use liquid extract, available at many natural foods stores. Instead of honey, we've used fruit juice-sweetened pancake syrup with wonderful results. It adds a fruity sweetness to this soy-based drink, which is great for breakfast.

1. Combine all ingredients in a blender or food processor and puree until smooth.

Calories per serving:	306
Grams of fat:	4.9
Percentage fat calories:	14%
Cholesterol:	0 mg.

Strawberry-Banana Smoothie

Serves 2

Prep Time: less than 5 minutes

1   **cup strawberry or other berry juice**

1   **pint fresh strawberries, washed and hulled**

¼   **cup nonfat dairy milk or 1% fat vanilla soy milk**

1   **banana, sliced**

1   **tablespoon nutritional yeast**

½   **teaspoon bee pollen granules**

This drink is the most luscious shade of pink imaginable. Kids will love it for a breakfast or snack, but it really tastes good enough to be dessert! You may want to substitute apple juice, but we especially like the combination of strawberry juice and fresh berries.

1. Combine all ingredients in a blender or food processor and puree until smooth.

Calories per serving:	282
Grams of fat:	1.6
Percentage fat calories:	5%
Cholesterol:	0 mg.

Carob Malted Soy Shake

Serves 4

Prep Time: less than 5 minutes

2   cups carob flavored 1% fat soy milk

2   cups orange juice

⅓   cup soft tofu

¼   cup carob powder

¼   cup honey

1   tablespoon lecithin powder

If you get cravings for those good old soda-fountain chocolate malts, this creamy beverage with its gentle orange undertone will make you wonder what you were missing. Plain, vanilla or another flavor of soy milk can be substituted here with equally delectable results.

1.   Combine all ingredients in a blender or food processor and blend 1 minute until smooth and frothy.

Calories per serving:	*206*
Grams of fat:	*3*
Percentage fat calories:	*17%*
Cholesterol:	*0 mg.*

Papaya Creamsicle Smoothie

Serves 2

Prep Time: less than 5 minutes

½   cup orange juice

1½ cups papaya concentrate

½   cup nonfat plain yogurt

1   teaspoon bee pollen

With the exotic tropical flavor of papaya concentrate and the velvety smoothness of yogurt, this lush drink provides plenty of vitamin C and natural fruit sugar for energy.

1. In a blender or food processor, combine all ingredients and blend until smooth and frothy.

Calories per serving:	*148*
Grams of fat:	*.2*
Percentage fat calories:	*1%*
Cholesterol:	*0 mg.*

Banana Colada

Serves 1

Prep Time: less than 5 minutes

1   **cup pineapple coconut juice**

1   **banana**

6   **ice cubes**

This luscious drink is our low-fat, nondairy version of a tropical shake. For an ultrasmooth drink, use a frozen banana.

1. Combine ingredients in a blender and puree until smooth.

Calories per serving:	*216*
Grams of fat:	*2.5*
Percentage fat calories:	*10%*
Cholesterol:	*0 mg.*

Spring Fever Blush

Serves 4

Prep Time: 5 minutes
Cooking Time: 5 minutes

2   raspberry herbal tea bags

1   12-ounce bottle vanilla
     soda or cola-flavored
     sparkling water

2   cups cherry cider

A tall tumbler of iced tea hits the spot on sunny days, and stress-free living definitely calls for caffeine-free tea. Fruit juice and sparkling water or natural soda make it slightly sweet and bubbly. Cherry cider gives this drink its charming blush, but you can mix and match natural herbal teas, flavored sparkling waters and juices to your heart's content.

1. Brew tea bags in 2 cups boiling water 5 minutes, then remove bags and let tea cool slightly.

2. Add soda and cider and mix well. Pour over ice and garnish with a berry or orange slice.

Calories per serving:	53
Grams of fat:	0
Percentage fat calories:	0%
Cholesterol:	0 mg.

Junebug

Serves 2

Prep Time: 5 minutes

1   **cup limeade or lime and white grape juice blend**

1   **cup kiwi juice or blend**

¼   **cup raspberry spritzer or sparkling juice blend**

    Handful of fresh raspberries

    Lime slices

Kiwi is all the rage in fruit juices and blends. We love the way kiwi and lime taste in tandem, with just a bit of raspberry for sweet tartness.

1.   Place a few ice cubes in two tall glasses and divide beverages between them. Garnish with a bamboo skewer of fresh raspberries and a slice of lime.

Calories per serving:	*141*
Grams of fat:	*0*
Percentage fat calories:	*0%*
Cholesterol:	*0 mg.*

Melon Delight

Serves 1

Prep Time: 5 minutes

1   small cantaloupe

²⁄₃   cup orange papaya juice

There are as many variations of this drink as there are types of melon. It can even be served right in the melon shell for a spectacular look.

1. Using a sharp knife, slice top off melon, reserving lid and cutting a zigzag pattern into upper edge. Cut a thin slice off bottom of melon so that it stands upright, taking care not to cut through shell. Scoop out the seeds and discard. Scoop out flesh and place it in a blender, then add juice and blend until smooth. Pour into melon shell and serve with straws.

Calories per serving:	*261*
Grams of fat:	*1.8*
Percentage fat calories:	*6%*
Cholesterol:	*0 mg.*

Indian Tea Punch

Serves 10

Prep Time: 15 minutes
Cooking Time: 5 minutes

4   lemon herbal tea bags

1   25.4-ounce bottle alcohol-free wine or sparkling cider

1   quart lemonade

    Limes or lemons, sliced

"Punch" originally came from the Hindi word "panch," meaning five. This signified the five traditional ingredients — lime, sugar, spices, water and a fermented sap called "arrack." The following combination is especially nice to serve at summer barbecues or family reunions, since it's not overly sweet. Make sure the ingredients are well chilled before combining.

1. Bring 4 cups water to a boil. Add tea bags and steep 5 to 10 minutes. Remove tea bags and cool at room temperature, then refrigerate.

2. To serve, combine tea, wine or cider and lemonade in a punch bowl. Garnish with slices of lemon or lime.

Calories per serving:	75
Grams of fat:	0
Percentage fat calories:	0%
Cholesterol:	0 mg.

Herbed Lemon Melonade

Serves 2

Prep Time: 5 minutes

1   **lemon herb tea bag**

1½ **cups melon juice**

½   **cup flavored sparkling water**

      Herb blossom ice cubes

Fresh herb blossoms and leaves like delicate rose geranium flowers add natural beauty and scent to any iced tea, spritzer or soda. Try freezing them in ice cubes to float in your favorite summer quencher. This basic formula can be varied with any complementary flavors of juice and herbal tea.

1. To make overnight without heating, place tea bag in juice and steep 12 hours. For a quicker drink, heat juice to just below boiling point and add tea bag. Steep 5 minutes and remove.

2. Let cool, pour into glasses and add sparkling water. Pop in a few herbed ice cubes and enjoy.

Calories per serving:	40
Grams of fat:	0
Percentage fat calories:	0%
Cholesterol:	0 mg.

Tomato Marimba

Serves 6

Prep Time: 5 minutes

2   12-ounce bottles alcohol-
    free beer

4   cups tomato-vegetable
    juice

1   teaspoon salt-free herb
    seasoning blend

    Juice of 2 limes

    **Dash of hot sauce, if
    desired**

    Celery stalks

    Sprigs of fresh cilantro

This drink's cool, crisp flavors make it perfect for quenching thirsts at summer brunches and other leisurely gatherings. The combination of alcohol-free beer and spicy tomato juice is sublime.

1. In a large pitcher, combine beer, juice, seasoning, lime juice and hot sauce, stirring well.

2. Pour into frosted mugs and garnish with a celery stalk and a sprig of fresh cilantro.

Calories per serving:	*113*
Grams of fat:	*0*
Percentage fat calories:	*0%*
Cholesterol:	*0 mg.*

Soy Spritzers

Strawberry Spritzer

Strawberry soy milk, strawberry nectar juice and lemon-flavored sparkling water.

Cherry Chocolate Fizz

Carob soy milk, cherry cider or juice and cherry-chocolate sparkling water.

Creamsicle

Vanilla soy milk, orange juice and orange-flavored sparkling water.

Black Un-Cow

Vanilla soy milk, black cherry juice and root beer or cola-flavored sparkling water.

Frothy soy spritzers are the result of marrying the refreshing qualities of fruit juice spritzers with the protein power of soy milk. A match made in heaven!

1. Fill a glass one-quarter full with soy milk. Add your choice of fruit juice to the halfway mark, then fill with flavored sparkling water. Stir briskly and enjoy immediately.

Hot Apple Flash

Serves 2

Prep Time: 7 minutes
Cooking Time: 5 minutes

1½ cups apple juice

2   tablespoons orange juice

2   tablespoons honey

1   teaspoon baking blend
     spice (or ⅓ teaspoon
     each cinnamon, nutmeg,
     allspice)

2   cinnamon sticks

2   large, ripe bananas

A trio of fruit flavors makes this naturally delicious.

1. In a saucepan, combine apple and orange juices with honey. Add spice blend and cinnamon sticks, cover and bring to a boil, then reduce heat and simmer 5 minutes.

2. In a blender, puree bananas. Remove cinnamon sticks from juice and pour juice into the blender. Blend until smooth and frothy. Pour into 2 glasses and garnish with cinnamon sticks.

Calories per serving:	438
Grams of fat:	1.4
Percentage fat calories:	3%
Cholesterol:	0 mg.

Hot Sparkling Cranberry Punch

Serves 8

Prep Time: 2 minutes
Cooking Time: 10 minutes

1	quart cranberry nectar
3	tablespoons honey, or to taste
1	tablespoon mulling spice blend
½	quart sparkling cider, at room temperature
1	orange, sliced

Honey softens the tartness of cranberries in this warming punch.

1. Combine cranberry nectar with honey in a large saucepan. Place mulling spice in tea ball or tie in cheesecloth and add to juice. Bring to a boil. Cover and remove from heat. Steep 10 minutes.

2. Transfer juice to a punch bowl. Add cider and sliced orange.

Calories per serving:	*123*
Grams of fat:	*0*
Percentage fat calories:	*0%*
Cholesterol:	*0 mg.*

Sleepyhead's Cafe Amaretto

Serves 1

Prep Time: 5 minutes

1 almond tea bag

1 cup prepared grain coffee or water-processed decaffeinated coffee

¼ cup nonfat dairy milk or 1% fat soy milk

1 teaspoon honey, or to taste

   Grated cinnamon

Here's a caffeine-free concoction for people who love the idea of lingering over after-dinner coffee but worry about losing sleep later on.

1. Add tea bag to hot coffee and let steep 2 minutes, then remove.

2. Add milk and honey and stir to combine.

3. Sprinkle with grated cinnamon before serving.

Calories per serving:	*51*
Grams of fat:	*.5*
Percentage fat calories:	*9%*
Cholesterol:	*0 mg.*

Glossary Of Natural Foods

A

Adzuki bean: A small, dark red bean native to the Orient.

Agar (also called agar-agar and kanten): A clear, flavorless, freeze-dried sea vegetable used like gelatin. Available in flakes or bars.

Amaranth: A tiny, mild-tasting grain and excellent source of high-quality protein. Whole seeds may be cooked like cereal, combined with other grains in side dishes and salads or added to baked goods. Amaranth flour may be substituted for up to half the wheat flour in baked goods.

Amazake: A sweet, creamy beverage made from brown rice.

Anasazi bean: A red and white speckled bean similar to pinto bean. Originally cultivated by Native Americans.

Arame: A thin, black, mild-tasting sea vegetable low in calories and high in minerals and trace elements, particularly iron, iodine and calcium. Arame must be boiled and softened before using. Excellent in salads and side dishes.

Arrowroot powder: A natural thickening agent extracted from the root of the arrowroot plant. May be substituted for cornstarch in sauces and puddings. Should be dissolved in cold water first to prevent lumping.

Arugula: A delicate, peppery flavored salad green that originated in Europe.

B

Balsamic vinegar: A sweet, full-bodied red wine vinegar. Delicious drizzled over salad greens for a fat-free, low-calorie dressing.

Bancha tea: Green tea made from the twigs and mature leaves of the tea plant. Contains less caffeine than other black or green teas.

Barley malt: A natural liquid sweetener made from sprouted barley. Similar color and consistency to molasses but has a milder flavor.

Basmati rice: A delicate, nutty-tasting variety of long grain rice that originated in India. It is typically polished white; however, brown basmati is also available.

C

Bee pollen: Granules of pollen are collected from bees as they pass through a screen covering the beehive entrance. Bee pollen is a concentrated source of protein and free amino acids.

Brown rice syrup: A thick syrup made from brown rice. Its mildly sweet taste is perfect in baked goods, desserts and sweets.

Cannellini: A small, white bean native to Italy.

Canola oil: Extracted from rapeseed, canola oil has the lowest saturated fat content of all commonly used cooking oils.

Capers: Buds of a flowering Mediterranean shrub that are pickled and used as a condiment.

Carob: A natural, low-fat substitute for chocolate in desserts and sweets. Produced by roasting and grinding locust tree pods. Available in powder, chips and syrup.

Chapati: An unleavened flat bread traditional in Indian cuisine similar to the Mexican wheat tortilla.

Cilantro: The pungent tasting leaf of the coriander plant; also referred to as Mexican or Chinese parsley.

Couscous: A refined grain product made by extracting the heart of the wheat kernel (semolina) and processing to create tiny pasta pellets. Whole-grain couscous is also available with the bran and germ intact.

D–F

Date sugar: Made by pulverizing dried dates, which are rich in natural sugars. Date sugar doesn't dissolve readily but is excellent in baked goods.

Egg replacer: Made from potato starch and tapioca. Fat and cholesterol-free egg replacer may be substituted for eggs in baked goods.

Fava bean: Light brown, flat, kidney-shaped bean popular in Italian and Middle Eastern cuisines.

G

Ghee (also called clarified butter): The clear yellow oil produced when sweet butter melts and separates. Frequently used in making curries.

Ginseng: A powerful herb long revered by the Chinese as an energy tonic.

Gomasio: A natural, low-sodium salt substitute made from ground, toasted sesame seeds mixed with sea salt in a 9:1 ratio.

Granulated cane juice: The dehydrated juice of organically grown sugar cane; less processed than sugar.

H–J

Hijiki: A dark brown, spaghettilike sea grass that has a strong ocean flavor, contains all the essential minerals and is especially high in calcium and iron. Hijiki is tasty in salads and side dishes but must be soaked and boiled before using.

Jicama: A crunchy, mildly sweet Mexican root vegetable shaped like a giant beet with tan skin and white flesh. Jicama may be peeled and eaten raw or cooked.

K–L

Kefir: A thick, fruit-flavored, cultured milk drink, kefir contains intestine-friendly bacteria and is a luscious substitute for milk-shakes.

Kombu: A thick, blackish-brown, broad-leaved sea vegetable used to flavor soups, stews and sauces. It may also be added to beans to reduce cooking time and improve digestibility. Kombu is rich in essential minerals, particularly calcium, phosphorus and potassium.

Kuzu: Natural thickening agent made from the Japanese kuzu plant. May be substituted for cornstarch or flour in sauces, soups and puddings.

Lecithin powder: A nutrition supplement extracted from soybeans; promotes fat metabolism.

M

Maple granules: A soft, granular sugar made by boiling down maple syrup. Maple granules give baked goods a distinctive flavor.

Millet: A small, yellow, beadlike grain, millet contains the most complete protein of all the grains. Whole millet may be cooked as a hot cereal or used in bread. Millet flour may be substituted for 25% of the whole wheat flour in baked goods.

Mirin: Sweet Japanese cooking wine made from rice; similar to sherry. Especially good in marinades, sauces and salad dressings.

Miso: Salted and fermented paste made from soy or other beans, or grains. Excellent as a base in soups and sauces or a flavor enhancer in dips and spreads. Miso is said to aid in the digestion of other foods.

Mung bean: Tiny, round, army-green bean native to the Orient. Often used sprouted in salads and stir-fries.

N–Q

Nori: Sea vegetables dried and pressed into thin sheets. Nori is used to wrap foods such as sushi. It's rich in calcium, iron, and vitamins A, B, and C.

Nutritional yeast: A natural flavor enhancer and nutrition supplement; rich in B vitamins, essential amino acids and chromium, which is important in sugar metabolism. Nutritional yeast imparts a "cheese" flavor to casseroles, soups and stews.

Quinoa: A small, disk-shaped grain that contains up to 50% more protein than common grains. It may be cooked whole and added to salads, soups and pilafs.

R

Radicchio: A purplish-red European lettuce with a pungent, slightly bitter flavor.

Rice vinegar: A mild, sweet vinegar made from rice. Excellent in salad dressings, marinades and sauces.

S

Sea salt: Made by evaporating ocean water. Unlike typical table salt, sea salt is high in other trace minerals besides just sodium chloride.

Shiitake: Large, full-flavored Japanese mushrooms with meaty texture. Delicious in soups, sauces and stir-fries.

Soba noodles: Japanese buckwheat noodles.

T

Tahini: A paste made from ground sesame seeds; consistency is similar to peanut butter. Use as a spread or stir into salad dressings, dips and sauces to add richness.

Tamari: Similar to soy sauce (shoyu), tamari is made by fermenting soybeans. Use in sauces and marinades and for seasoning soups and stir-fries.

Teff: The smallest whole grain, teff is a rich source of calcium, protein and iron. It may be eaten as a cooked cereal or added to baked goods.

Tempeh: Cracked whole soybeans that have been cooked, fermented and steamed. High in protein and vitamin B-12, tempeh is an excellent substitute for meat.

Texturized vegetable protein (TVP®): A high-protein, low-fat, cholesterol-free food product made from soybeans. Available in granules, flakes and chunks, TVP® is an excellent substitute for meat in chilis, stews and casseroles.

Tofu: Curd that results when ground soybeans are cooked, drained and pressed into cubes. Available in soft, regular or firm texture. Tofu is abundant in protein, lysine, calcium and iron.

U–Z

Umeboshi: Salt-pickled Japanese plums; available whole, in a paste or vinegar.

Udon noodles: Japanese wheat and rice pasta.

Wakame: A thick, dark green sea vegetable, mild-tasting wakame is especially good in soups, stews and salads. It's rich in calcium and trace minerals.

Wasabi (also called Japanese horseradish): Derived from the green flesh of the Japanese wasabi root. In the U.S. wasabi is available in powder form which must be reconstituted with water. It has a fresh, biting flavor and is commonly used as a condiment for sushi.

Delicious! Recipe Index

The Delicious! Collection
Simple Recipes For Healthy Living
ORDER FORM

If *The Delicious! Collection* is unavailable at your local store, you may purchase it directly from New Hope Communications. Please complete the form below and return it along with payment to:

The Delicious! Collection, New Hope Communications, 1301 Spruce Street, Boulder, Colorado 80302
Telephone 303-939-8440 FAX 303-939-9559

The Delicious! Collection $16.95 each   Quantity _____   **Total** _____

Tax, Colorado residents: City of Boulder, 6.66%; Denver-Metro area
(RTD District), 3.8%; Outside Denver-Metro area, 3.0%   **Tax** _____

Shipping & Handling, 1-2 copies: Continental U.S., $3.00;
Hawaii and Alaska, $4.00; Canada, $5.00   **Shipping & Handling** _____

Please make check payable in U.S. funds to New Hope Communications.   **TOTAL** _____

Payment method: ❑ Check   ❑ MasterCard   ❑ VISA   Card # _____   Exp. Date _____

Cardholder Name: _____   Signature: _____
Please print name as it appears on card

Ship to: _____
NAME   TELEPHONE

Address: _____
STREET   CITY   STATE   ZIP

Delicious! Your Magazine Of Natural Living
ORDER FORM

Many natural and health foods stores in the United States give copies of *Delicious! Magazine* to their customers at no charge. If you are unable to find *Delicious! Magazine* in your area, annual subscriptions are available for $20.00.*
Delicious! Magazine is published 8 times per year.

Please send a check payable to New Hope Communications in the amount of $20.00 to: *Delicious! Magazine* Subscription Dept., New Hope Communications, 1301 Spruce Street, Boulder, CO 80302, Telephone: 303-939-8440 FAX 303-939-9559

Name _____   Telephone _____

Address _____   City _____   State _____   Zip _____

Canadian subscriptions are $24.00 (in U.S. dollars and drawn on a U.S. bank).